Cook Indian

P. Majumder

Photographs by:
Andrew Merewether

TIMES BOOKS
International

Contents

Desserts

Savouries

Introduction

Tasting Indian cooking is an adventure, but attempting to cook Indian is a whole new experience. Indian dishes need not be hot - you may still taste the exotic, savoury delights of Indian food without the tortuous lip-burning by just cutting down on the proportion of curry powder or chillies used. The challenge and excitement in Indian cooking is enough to tempt even the least adventurous of housewives to try out one or two Indian dishes in her kitchen.

You've heard of (and most likely enjoyed) Tandoori Chicken, Naan, Roti Paratha, Mutton Biryani, Spicy (Indian) Mutton Soup ..... why not try them out yourselves.

This book attempts to give a balanced selection of as many Indian delicacies as possible, to keep you busy. There are hot and mild curries, spicy chicken dishes and those requiring no spices at all (for example, Chicken Mailu and Parsi Roast Chicken), the Indian style "cutlets", the delightful kababs, and desserts and cocktails a-la-Indian from puddings to sherbets. And with the guidance of the author, who has had more than forty years of experience in Indian cooking and teaching the art, you can be confident of turning out some fine Indian dishes.

You haven't had spice in your life until you've savoured the spice in Indian cooking! Have fun!

Acknowledgement

The author would like to express her thanks to all her friends who have helped her in the preparation of dishes for the photography sessions and Aw Pottery for the loan of utensils.

Notes

Rice

Rice, staple food of the Indians, is normally eaten plain-boiled, with other dishes. It may be fried in ghee with raisins, nuts and spices (pillau) or cooked with meats, vegetables and spices (biryani). "Basmati" rice is the long-grained, expensive variety ("basmati" means "flavoured") but Patna rice may be used instead of it.

To get pillau rice : After rice has been fried, water and milk should be added to 1 inch (2½ cm) above the rice level. One way of measuring is to dip the index finger in to the first joint. This should be the amount of water to be absorbed. Firstly, cook the rice on medium heat until it is three-quarters cooked, by which time three-quarters of the water should be absorbed. Then, continue cooking on low heat or in a slow oven till all the water has been absorbed and rice is cooked. When cooked with lentils (khitchri dishes) a little more water should be added to get the "correct" consistency.

Oil

Vegetable oils are normally used in Indian cooking as they are "unflavoured" or "tasteless". In the making of pickles however, either mustard or olive oil is preferred.

Channa (soft cream milk)

Mix 2 tablespoons vinegar with 2 cups water and add this to heated milk. Stir slowly until the milk curdles and strain this mixture through a piece of fine muslin cloth. Set aside for 5 minutes. Wash the residue under a running tap and tie the muslin cloth into a bag. Hang this up to dry till all moisture has been drained.

Garam masala

This is obtained by mixing together 1 tablespoon cinnamon, ¼ tablespoon clove and one-third tablespoon cardamom.

Dhal (lentils)

A common Indian delicacy, dhal dishes are often eaten with rice or breads ("roti" in Indian). Unless pre-cleaned and packaged, dhals usually require thorough cleaning before cooking. Firstly, look out for "spoilt" grains and little stones or gravel. Then, wash several times with water to remove remaining dirt. Types of dhal: Gram dhal or channa dhal is the largest type of lentils. Mysore dhal is the small and red variety. Kabuli, channa or horse gram dhal is the large split pea and urhad dhal is the black type. Green (moong dhal) or black split peas may be washed and boiled without first frying them and may be mixed with vegetables.

Ghee

Ghee is butter clarified by boiling. Ghee may be bought in tins from supermarkets.

On chops, cutlets and kababs

Chops are rounded, like oranges or eggs. Cutlets are flat, and for kababs, the meat is pounded after frying.

Soft Khoa

This is obtained by slowly bringing cow's milk to a boil, then allowing it to simmer over low heat stirring continuously till a ball is obtained.
Dry khoa is obtained by gently boiling soft khoa till a powder form is obtained.

Weights and measures

In this book, all metric equivalents of imperial weights and measures are shown in parenthesis, e.g. —
½ lb (225 g)
1 lb (450 g)
1 in (2½ cm)

Some basic equivalents

Imperial	Metric
1 oz	28 g
1 lb	450 g or ½ kg
1 pint	½ litre
1 in	2½ cm

Cups

The author, being a traditionalist, uses a teacup as a measure of 1 cup, which is approximately two-thirds of a metric cup.

Rice and Breads

Plain Pillau

Serves: 4

1 pound (450 g) long grain *Patna* Rice
1 cup ghee *or* melted butter
1 tablespoon chopped almonds
1 tablespoon raisins
2 onions, sliced
2 sticks cinnamon
6 pods cardamom
1 teaspoon sugar
salt to taste
1 tablespoon ginger juice
2 teaspoons saffron
2-3 bay leaves
1 cup evaporated milk
3 tablespoons green peas
2 teaspoons rose water

Wash rice, then leave in a colander for 10 minutes to drain well.

Heat ghee or butter in a pot and fry almonds and raisins till brown. Remove to a dish. Fry onions in the same oil until golden brown. Remove and set aside.

Fry cinnamon and cardamom in the same oil. Add rice, sugar, salt, ginger juice and saffron and fry till rice is lightly browned. Then add bay leaves and milk.

Pour in sufficient water to bring the liquid level to 1 inch (2½ cm) above the rice level. Cover the pot and cook on medium heat, stirring occasionally. When three-quarters of the water has been absorbed, add green peas and rose water.

Continue to cook over very low heat, or add a little ghee on top and cook in a slow oven, till all the water has been absorbed.

Serve pillau garnished with fried almonds, raisins and onions. Serve with any curry or *kabab.*

Chicken Pillau

Serves: 8

2 pounds (900 g) long grain *Patna* rice
1 chicken, about 2 pounds (900 g)
salt to taste
2 teaspoons ground turmeric
½ cup yoghurt
½ pound (225 g) ghee
4 cloves garlic, chopped
5 onions, sliced
3 teaspoons ginger juice
1 tablespoon ground chilli
2 tablespoons cummin, ground or whole
2 teaspoons sugar
¼ pound (110 g) cashew-nuts
1 tablespoon raisins
2 sticks cinnamon
8 pods cardamom
1 cup milk, evaporated
2-3 bay leaves

Wash rice and leave in a colander for 10 minutes to drain.

Clean, wash and cut chicken into big pieces. Rub with salt, ground turmeric and yoghurt and leave for 1 hour.

Heat a saucepan, add a little ghee and fry garlic and half the sliced onions for a few minutes. Add ½ cup water, ginger juice, ground chilli, ground cummin and sugar. Stir until liquid dries up. Add chicken, stir well till some juice is released, then cover the pan and cook on very low heat, stirring occasionally. If the liquid dries up, add a little water. When the chicken is three-quarters cooked (the gravy should be almost dry by this time), remove from heat.

In a clean saucepan, heat a little ghee and fry cashew-nuts and raisins till brown. Remove to a dish. In the same oil, fry the remaining sliced onions till brown. Set this aside.

Transfer the ghee to a deeper pot and fry cinnamon and cardamom. Add rice and fry till it is slightly browned. Add milk, bay leaves, chicken and sufficient water to bring the liquid level up to 1 inch (2 ½ cm) above the level of the ingredients. Cover the pan and cook over medium heat, stirring occasionally, till three-quarters of the liquid is absorbed by the rice. Reduce heat to very low, add the remaining ghee, cover and cook till dry.

Sprinkle with cashew-nuts, raisins and fried onion slices.

Serve with a salad and *chutney*.

Prawn Pillau

Serves: 4

1 pound (450 g) *Basmati* **rice**
1 pound (450 g) big prawns
salt to taste
2 teaspoons ground turmeric
½ cup ghee *or* **oil**
1 tablespoon cashew-nuts
5 onions, sliced
4 cloves garlic, chopped
1 tablespoon ground chilli
2 teaspoons ground cummin
2 teaspoons ground sweet cummin
2 teaspoons sugar
2-3 sticks cinnamon
6 pods cardamom
2 teaspoons ginger juice
2 cups coconut milk
2-3 green chillies, sliced

Wash rice and leave in a colander to drain for 10 minutes. Shell and devein prawns, wash with salt water to remove sliminess, then rub with salt and ground turmeric.

Heat a little ghee in a saucepan and brown cashew-nuts. Remove and set aside. Brown sliced onions in the same ghee. Remove half the onions to a dish, then add prawns, garlic, ground chilli, ground cummin, ground sweet cummin, and 1 teaspoon sugar to the pan. Stir-fry for a few minutes and remove from heat.

Heat ¾ cup ghee or oil in a pot, then add cinnamon, cardamom, rice, salt, 1 teaspoon sugar and ginger juice. Fry till the rice is slightly browned, then add coconut milk and prawns. Add sufficient water to raise the level of liquid to 1 inch (2½ cm) above the level of ingredients. Cover the pan and cook over medium heat, stirring occasionally.

When most of the liquid has been absorbed, add the remaining ghee and finish cooking over very low heat. When rice is completely dry, remove from heat and mix in the cashew-nuts, green chilli and fried onions. Serve with a salad.

Peshowari Pillau

Serves : 10

3 pounds (900 g) *Basmati* rice
4 bay leaves
2 sticks cinnamon
4 pods cardamom
6 cloves
salt to taste
2 teaspoons sugar
1 teaspoon ground turmeric
1 cup evaporated milk
3 cups *yakhni* water*
½ pound roasted *moong dhal* (green split bean)
1 pound (450 g) cooked mutton chops†
5 onions, sliced
1 tablespoon chopped almonds
1 tablespoon raisins
½ pound (225 g) ghee *or* butter

*Yakhni water

3 cloves garlic, peeled and left whole
2 inch (5 cm) piece ginger, sliced
2 tablespoons *channa dhal*
1 tablespoon sweet cummin
8 dried chillies
2 sticks cinnamon
8 pods cardamom
8 cloves
4 bay leaves
1 teaspoon salt

†Mutton Chops

1 pound (450 g) mutton chops
4 cloves garlic, sliced
2 onions, sliced
1 teaspoon sugar
1 teaspoon ground turmeric
½ cup yoghurt
1 cup *yakhni* water
1 cup hot water
salt to taste
1 tablespoon ghee

*Yakhni water

Wash the ingredients for *yakhni* water and wrap loosely in a muslin bag. Boil 10 cups water in a saucepan, drop in the bag of spices and other ingredients and simmer on very low heat till only 4 cups water remain. Remove from heat.

†Mutton chops

Cut mutton into fairly large ½ inch (1 cm) thick pieces. Heat 1 tablespoon ghee in a pan over medium heat and brown garlic and onions. Put in mutton pieces, salt, sugar and ground turmeric and fry for 15 minutes or till liquid dries up. Then add yoghurt, *yakhni* water and hot water. Stir to mix ingredients. Cover and allow to simmer till meat is three-quarters cooked. This will take about 30 minutes, if you use a pressure cooker. Remove pan from heat.

Pillau

Wash *Basmati* rice and leave in a sieve or colander for 10 minutes to drain well.

Heat ¼ pound (110 g) ghee or butter in a saucepan and fry bay leaves, cinnamon, cardamom and cloves for a few minutes. Add rice, salt, sugar and ground turmeric and stir continuously till rice is light brown before adding milk, *yakhni* water, *dhal* and cooked mutton. Cover the pan after stirring to mix ingredients and keep on medium heat, stirring frequently to prevent burning.

When most of the water has been absorbed, turn heat down to low and spread remaining ghee or butter over the rice. The pillau should be cooked dry in 20 minutes. Fry onions, almonds and raisins in a little ghee till brown and sprinkle over pillau. Serve pillau hot with *chutney* and salad.

Mutton Biryani

Oven setting : 110°C, 225°F, Gas Regulo 1
Serves   : 8

2 pounds (900 g) mutton
salt to taste
1 teaspoon sugar
1½ tablespoons ground chilli
½ cup yoghurt
2 teaspoons ground coriander
2 teaspoons ground cummin
2 teaspoons ground turmeric
2 tablespoons ginger juice
2 teaspoons vinegar
½ pound (225 g) ghee *or* butter oil
8 cloves garlic, chopped
2-3 sticks cinnamon
8 pods cardamom
10 cloves
6 onions, sliced
2 pounds (900 g) *Basmati* rice
  (or good quality rice)
2 teaspoons saffron
½ cup milk
2 tablespoons cashew-nuts

Cut mutton into fairly large ½ inch (1 cm) pieces. Marinate in a mixture of salt, sugar, ground chilli, yoghurt, ground coriander, ground cummin, ground turmeric, ginger juice and vinegar. Leave mutton in the marinade for 45 minutes.

Heat 3 teaspoons ghee in a saucepan and fry garlic, cinnamon, cardamom, cloves and half the quantity of sliced onions for a few minutes. Then add mutton and stir well before covering the pan. When liquid has dried up and mutton is almost cooked, remove from heat.

While mutton is left in the marinade, wash rice and boil in water with 1 teaspoon salt over medium heat. Water level should be about 1 inch (2½ cm) above the rice level. When rice is almost cooked, drain off remaining water and spread on a flat dish to cool.

Mix saffron with 2 teaspoons hot milk and stir into the rice. Put the rice in a large pan and add the almost cooked mutton. Pour most of the remaining ghee over the meat. Cook in a slow oven.

In a clean frying pan, heat the little ghee left and fry the remaining onions till crispy. Remove onions to a dish and brown cashew-nuts in the same oil. Mix fried cashew-nuts and onions with biryani before serving.

Vegetable Khitchri

Serves: 6

1 pound (450 g) *Basmati* rice
1 ½ pounds (675 g) *moong dhal* (green split bean)
½ pound (225 g) potatoes
1 pound (450 g) cauliflower
½ cup ghee *or* oil
½ teaspoon cummin seeds
2 sticks cinnamon
6 pods cardamom
1 inch (2 ½ cm) piece ginger, chopped
2-3 bay leaves
1 tablespoon ground chilli
1 tablespoon ground cummin
1 teaspoon ground turmeric
2 teaspoons sugar
salt to taste
20 shallots, peeled and left whole
2 red chillies, finely sliced
3 dried chillies, each cut into 2-3 sections
4 onions, sliced
1 cup green peas
2 teaspoons *garam masala*

Wash rice and *dhal.* Cut potatoes and cauliflower into bite-sized pieces. Fry the pieces in oil till half-cooked, then remove from heat.

Heat a little ghee or oil in a large saucepan and add cummin seeds, cinnamon, cardamom, ginger and bay leaves. Fry for a few minutes before adding rice, *dhal,* ground chilli, ground cummin, ground turmeric, sugar and salt. Mix well, then add 6 cups water and cook covered over medium heat.

When rice is half-cooked, add potatoes, cauliflower, shallots and red chillies. Cover the pan once again and simmer over medium heat till rice is cooked. Remove from heat.

In a clean pan, fry dried chillies, sliced onions and peas. Add these and *garam masala* to the rice and mix thoroughly before serving.

(clockwise) — Mutton Shahi Korma, Pineapple Chutney, Calcutta Paratha.
(Recipes: pp. 59, 88, 14)

(clockwise) Channa Dhal, Mutton Cutlet, Fish Cutlet, Stuffed Cabbage
(Recipes: pp. 21, 30, 29, 22)

Top right — Doh Piaji, Vegetable Dhal
Left — Sweet Sour Lamb
(Recipes: pp. 23, 24, 67)

(clockwise) — Nimki, Samosas, Cheese Cutlet, Tamarind Chutney
(Recipes: pp. 18, 113, 28, 88)

Chicken Khitchri

Serves: 6

2 pounds (900 g) *Basmati* rice
2½ pounds (1125 g) *moong dhal*
2 pounds (900 g) chicken
salt to taste
2 teaspoons ground turmeric
¾ cup ghee *or* oil
5 cloves garlic, chopped
6 onions, sliced
1 tablespoon ground chilli
3 teaspoons ground cummin
2 teaspoons sugar
1 teaspoon cummin
3 sticks cinnamon
8 pods cardamom
2-3 bay leaves
12 shallots, peeled and left whole
2-3 green chillies, each cut into 2-3 pieces
1 inch piece ginger, chopped
1 teaspoon *garam masala*
1 cup cooked green peas

Wash rice and *dhal.* Cut chicken into 8 pieces and rub these with salt and ground turmeric.

Heat 1 tablespoon ghee in a saucepan and brown garlic and half the sliced onions, then add chicken, ground chilli, ground cummin and 1 teaspoon sugar. Stir till meat juices are released, then cover the pan and cook over medium heat. When the liquid dries, add a little water and cook till chicken is tender. Remove to a dish.

Heat most of the remaining ghee in a large pot and fry cummin seeds, cinnamon, cardamom and remaining sliced onions for a few minutes. Then add rice, *dhal,* salt and 1 teaspoon sugar. Stir till *dhal* and rice are slightly browned, then add bay leaves, chicken, 12 cups of water and cover the pot. Simmer over medium heat. When rice and *dhal* are almost cooked, add shallots and fresh chillies and simmer till *dhal* and rice are cooked.

In a clean pan, heat the rest of the ghee and fry dried chillies and chopped ginger for a few minutes. Stir in *garam masala* and green peas. Mix this thoroughly with the khitchri. Serve hot with fried foods.

Moglai Khitchri

Serves: 4

1 ½ pounds (675 g) *moong dhal*
1 pound (450 g) *Basmati* rice
1 pound (450 g) mutton
2 teaspoons ground turmeric
½ cup yoghurt
2 teaspoons ground coriander
1 tablespoon ground chilli
2 teaspoons vinegar
2 teaspoons sugar
2 teaspoons salt
6 cloves garlic, chopped
5 onions, sliced
1 teaspoon cummin
2 sticks cinnamon
5 pods cardamom
2 teaspoons chopped ginger
3 eggs, beaten
1 teaspoon *garam masala*
10 shallots, peeled and left whole
½ cup ghee *or* oil

Fry *dhal* till brown (without oil). Wash and drain well. Then wash rice and drain well. Cut mutton into ½ inch (1 cm) thick pieces and marinate in a mixture of 1 teaspoon ground turmeric, yoghurt, ground coriander and chilli, vinegar, 1 teaspoon sugar and 1 teaspoon salt. Leave meat in the marinade for 2 hours.

Heat 1 tablespoon ghee in a pan over medium heat and fry garlic and half the onion slices for 5 minutes. Add mutton and stir for 10 minutes, then cover the pan and cook over low heat till no liquid remains. Add ½ cup water, stir well and cover once more to simmer. When mutton is three-quarters cooked, remove from heat.

Heat remaining ghee in a large pan and fry cummin, cinnamon, cardamom and remaining onion slices for 5 minutes before adding rice, 1 teaspoon turmeric, ginger, 1 teaspoon sugar and 1 teaspoon salt. Stir till rice is light brown, then add mutton pieces, fried *dhal* and 6 cups cold water. Cover and cook over medium heat till rice is almost cooked, then add beaten eggs, *garam masala* and shallots. Continue cooking over low heat, stirring frequently to prevent burning, till rice grains are tender. Serve hot with fried fish or fried vegetables.

Wholemeal Flour Chapati

Makes: 20

1 pound (450 g) wholewheat flour
¼ pound plain flour
1 teaspoon salt
1 tablespoon margarine *or* ghee
1 ½ cups lukewarm water

Put aside about ¼ cup flour for dusting the work surface and balls of dough and put the rest in a mixing bowl. Mix salt with both types of flour, then rub in ghee or margarine. Add water a little at a time, kneading all the while. When all the water has been added, continue kneading for at least 10 minutes to get a soft dough. Wrap this in a damp tea towel or a piece of muslin and let it stand for 2-3 hours. Chapatis are lighter if the dough is left to stand overnight.

Shape half a handful of dough into a ball. Flatten slightly and dust with flour. Roll out evenly on a lightly floured board into flat, round shapes about ⅛ inch (3 mm) thick.

After rolling out all the chapatis, heat a heavy frying pan or a *tawa* over medium heat. When it is smoking hot, place a chapati on it for about a minute. Bubbles will start to rise after half a minute. Turn the chapati over and press gently with a small cloth or towel. When this side has also risen, both sides should have brown spots. Remove from the pan and keep in a covered bowl or flat dish. Serve with vegetable or meat curries.

Milk Chapati

Makes: 16

1 pound (450 g) plain white flour
½ pound (225 g) wholewheat flour
1 teaspoon baking powder
5 teaspoons castor sugar
1 teaspoon pepper
1 teaspoon salt, or to taste
3 ounces (90 g) butter *or* ghee
1 egg, beaten
1 cup thin milk *or* thick coconut milk

Leave aside ¼ cup wholewheat flour for dusting the working surface. Sieve white and the remaining wholewheat flour with baking powder, castor sugar, pepper and salt into a mixing bowl. Rub in melted butter and a beaten egg. Adding a little milk at a time, knead well to obtain a soft dough.

Divide the dough into 16 equal portions and shape each into a ball. Flatten slightly and dust with flour, then roll out into thin round shapes, on a lightly floured board.

Heat a frying pan or *tawa* over low heat. Fry one side of chapati till light brown, then turn over and brown the other side. A little butter may be rubbed on the chapati while cooking. Keep chapatis in a covered bowl and serve with vegetable curry.

Calcutta Paratha

Makes: 10

1 ½ pounds (675 g) plain white flour
½ pound (225 g) ghee
1 teaspoon salt
2 teaspoons castor sugar
1 ½ teaspoons baking powder
2 eggs, beaten
1 cup thin milk *or* cold water
½ cup cornflour for sprinkling

Mix flour with melted ghee, salt, castor sugar, baking powder and eggs. Knead well, adding milk or water a little at a time. The kneading is important and should take at least 10 minutes. Wrap in a damp tea towel and let the dough stand for 2-3 hours.

Divide the dough into 10 equal portions and shape into balls. Keep the balls of dough covered with a damp cloth and take out one at a time to work with. Flatten slightly and roll out into a very thin circle, dabbing with a little ghee if necessary. Mix 2 tablespoons ghee with 2 tablespoons cornflour and spread a little of this mixture over the paratha before folding it.

The paratha can be folded in many ways — one way gives a triangular shape, another a round one. First, the triangle: fold over once to get a semicircle, then fold in half again to obtain a triangle. Dust with a little flour again, then roll out each side so that the triangle becomes twice as large. Do not press too hard or the air trapped by the folding will escape. The triangle should be thicker than the original circle. If you wish to obtain a circle after folding, make a cut from the centre of the paratha to the edge. Starting with the cut edge, roll around so that you obtain a cone. Pick it up and let it stand on its base. Push the apex towards the base so that a circular lump of dough is obtained once again, and roll out gently, this time to a smaller, slightly thicker circle.

Heat a little ghee on a frying pan or *tawa* over medium heat. Place a paratha on it. As soon as one side is brown, turn it over. This time, add a little ghee to the paratha to make it crispy. The parathas should be golden brown. If they turn out too dark, adjust the heat.

Serve with vegetable curries.

Note: If you wish to cook parathas early, wrap each in aluminium foil and heat for 10 minutes in a moderate oven (300 °F or 150 °C) before serving.

Moglai Paratha

Makes: 20

2 tablespoons ghee *or* oil
1 pound (450 g) minced mutton
6 onions, chopped
4 cloves garlic, chopped
1 tablespoon ground chilli
1 teaspoon sugar
2 green chillies, chopped
2 teaspoons ginger juice
1 teaspoon roasted ground cummin
2 teaspoons chopped roasted almonds
1 teaspoon *garam masala*
2 teaspoons chopped coriander leaves
salt to taste

Dough

2 pounds (900 g) plain white flour
¼ pound (110 g) wholewheat flour
2 tablespoons ghee
1 teaspoon baking powder
1½ teaspoons salt
½ cup yoghurt
3 eggs, beaten
1 cup milk
1 cup ghee for frying

Heat 2 tablespoons ghee in a pan and fry mutton mixed with onions, garlic, ground chilli, sugar, green chillies and ginger juice. After a few minutes, add 1 cup water. When simmering, add ground cummin, almonds, *garam masala*, coriander and salt to taste. Cook till dry.

Put aside about ½ cup white flour for dusting the working surface and put the rest in a mixing bowl. Rub 1 tablespoon ghee, baking powder, salt, yoghurt and beaten eggs into the flour. Knead well, adding a little milk at a time. After about 10 minutes, when the dough is soft from kneading, wrap in a damp tea towel and let it stand for 4 hours.

Divide the dough into 20 equal portions and shape into balls. Keep the balls covered with a damp cloth and take out one at a time to work with. Flatten slightly, then roll out into a circle about ⅛ inch (3 mm) thick on a floured surface. Place a portion of the mutton mixture on one side of the paratha and spread so that one semi-circle is covered with mutton. Fold the uncovered half over the half covered with mutton and roll out thinly.

Heat a frying pan or *tawa* on medium heat, and place the paratha on it. Turn over several times to cook evenly. When half-cooked, spread a little ghee on it and fry till lightly browned. Serve hot with a *chutney*.

Naan

Baking   : 10 mins
Oven setting: 150°, 300°F, Gas Regulo 4
Makes   : 6

¼ teaspoon dry yeast
¼ cup warm water *or* warm, thin milk
1 teaspoon sugar
1 tablespoon yoghurt
1 teaspoon baking powder
1 egg, beaten
2 teaspoons melted ghee
½ teaspoon salt
2 cups plain white flour
2 teaspoons black cummin seeds

Sprinkle yeast in ¼ cup warm water. Stir in sugar and leave for about 10 minutes. If the yeast is active, it should start to froth. (If not, begin again with a fresh lot of yeast, sugar and warm water.) Mix with yoghurt till smooth, then stir in baking powder, beaten egg, 2 teaspoons melted ghee and salt.

Put the flour in a bowl, make a well in the centre and pour in the liquid mixture. Rub in till well mixed and knead for about 10 minutes till the dough is somewhat elastic. Shape into a ball, brush with a little melted ghee and leave covered with a damp cloth in a warmed bowl. It will rise to double its size in about 4 hours.

Knead for a couple of minutes once more, then divide the dough into 6 portions. Shape into balls and leave in a bowl covered by a damp cloth for 10 minutes. While waiting, preheat the oven to very hot (500°F or 260°C) and lightly grease 2 or 3 baking sheets.

Heat a griddle over very low heat and place one ball of dough on it. Flatten, then stretch one side out into a teardrop shape. Stretch and pat till you have a teardrop shape about 6 inches (15 cm) long and 4 inches (10 cm) wide at one end. Brush the top with a little melted butter or ghee and sprinkle with black cummin seeds.

Place about 2 or 3 naan on a baking sheet and bake for about 10 minutes in a moderately hot oven. They should be puffed and have a crisp and golden skin. If not sufficiently browned, put under a hot grill for a couple of minutes. Serve hot with Tandoori Chicken or *kababs* and *chutney.*

Potato Bora

Makes : 12

1 pound (450 g) potatoes, cooked and mashed
3 tablespoons rice flour
1 egg, beaten
2 onions, finely chopped
2 green chillies, chopped
2 teaspoons ground chilli
2-3 teaspoons chopped coriander leaves
½ teaspoon sugar
salt to taste
oil for deep-fat frying
1 teaspoon cummin
¼ cup ground fried peanuts

Mix mashed potato with water and all other ingredients, except oil.

Shape into little balls.

Make a hollow in each ball and put in ground peanuts and deep-fry till golden brown. Drain well and serve with fried onion rings, chilli and tomato sauces.

Cream Bread

Baking   : 20 mins
Oven setting: 100°C, 200°F, Gas Regulo 1
Makes   : 6

1 cup plain white flour
¼ cup rice flour
4 ounces (110 g) butter
½ cup castor sugar
1 egg yolk (beaten)
3 tablespoons cream (beaten)
1 teaspoon baking powder
½ tablespoon vanilla essence

Warm plain white flour and rice flour in a clean dry pan. Sieve and set aside to cool. When cool, place flour in a bowl and rub in butter. Add castor sugar, egg yolk, cream, baking powder and vanilla essence. Knead well to get a stiff dough.

Roll out to ¼ inch (½ cm) thickness on a floured surface and cut into small rounds using a 2 inch (5 cm) cutter. Prick well with a fork. Place the rounds on a greased tray and bake in a moderately hot oven for about 20 minutes or till light golden. Sprinkle with sugar and leave on the trays to cool before storing.

Dhal Tikara

Makes : 12

½ pound (225 g) *channa dhal*
1 cup ghee
½ teaspoon cummin
4 green chillies, chopped
4 onions, sliced
2 teaspoons sugar
salt to taste
2 teaspoons ginger juice
2 teaspoons ground chilli
2 teaspoons chopped coriander leaves
2 teaspoons roasted ground cummin
1 pound (450 g) plain white flour
½ pound (225 g) wholemeal flour

Boil *dhal* in 4 cups water for 30 minutes till three-quarters cooked. Heat 1 tablespoon ghee in a pan over medium heat and fry cummin, chopped green chillies and onion slices for 10 minutes. Add *dhal*, sugar, salt to taste, ginger juice, ground chilli and chopped coriander leaves. Stir-fry for 15 minutes or till *dhal* is tender and almost dry. Add roasted ground cummin and remove from heat.

Put both kinds of flour in a large mixing bowl. Rub in 2 tablespoons ghee, then slowly add a little cold water, kneading well to get a soft dough. Divide the dough into 24 lumps. Shape into balls and flatten slightly. Roll out into circles about $^1/_{10}$ inch (3 mm) thick.

Spread some *dhal* mixture centrally on 12 circles of dough, leaving about ½ inch (1 cm) dough around the edge clear. Place the remaining 12 circles of dough on these 12, sandwiching the *dhal* mixture between. Press the edges together and roll out a little.

Heat a frying pan or griddle over medium heat. Fry tikara one at a time till slightly browned. Spread 2 teaspoons ghee on the upper surface of tikara and turn over. Fry this side for 2-3 minutes before removing from heat. Serve with any *chutney* or vegetable dish.

Rogni Roti

Makes: 6

½ pound (225 g) wholewheat flour
½ pound (225 g) plain white flour
2 teaspoons baking powder
4 ounces (110 g) cream (beaten)
5 ounces (140 g) ghee
2 teaspoons sugar
salt to taste
1 cup milk
extra melted ghee

Sieve both kinds of flour together. Add baking powder and rub in cream, ghee, sugar and salt. Make a well in the centre of this mixture and pour in about half the milk. Mix with the flour and knead welll, adding milk slowly as you work with the dough. After kneading about 10 minutes, leave in a bowl covered with a damp cloth for 4 hours.

Shape dough into lumps the size of eggs and roll out on a floured board into flat triangular shapes. They need not be very regular. Bake in a hot griddle till light brown. Remove from griddle and brush with a little melted ghee. Serve with any curry.

Nimki

Makes: 12

½ pound (225 g) plain white flour
¼ pound (110 g) ghee *or* corn oil
2 teaspoons lemon juice
1 teaspoon baking powder
1 teaspoon salt
1 cup cold water

Put flour in a mixing bowl. Rub 1 ½ tablespoons ghee, lemon juice, baking powder and salt into the flour. Make a well in the centre of the flour mixture and add half the cold water. Work flour into this well and knead, adding the rest of the water gradually to make a soft dough.

Divide the dough into egg-sized lumps and roll out into thin round shapes on a lightly floured board. Fold each into a semi-circle, then fold once again to obtain a little triangle. Prick all over with a fork.

Heat the remaining ghee in a pan and deep-fry nimki on low heat till the pieces rise and are lightly browned. Drain well before serving with *chutney.*

Loochi

Makes: 30

1 pound (450 g) plain white flour
¼ pound (110 g) wholewheat flour
½ pound (225 g) ghee *or* corn oil
1 teaspoon salt
1 teaspoon castor sugar
1 ½ cups cold water

Put both kinds of flour in a mixing bowl. Rub in 4 teaspoons melted ghee, salt and sugar. Make a well in the centre and add 1 cup water. Work flour into this well and knead till dough is quite dry. After kneading about 10 minutes, add 1 tablespoon ghee and knead again to make a soft dough. Divide the dough into egg-sized lumps and roll out into thin round shapes on a lightly floured surface.

Heat the remaining ghee in a pan and fry loochis one at a time over medium heat. Press loochi down with a perforated spoon until it begins to rise. When it has risen, turn it over and cook till light golden. Drain well and serve hot with honey, butter or meat curry.

Vegetables

Cauliflower in Yoghurt

Serves: 8

3 pounds (1350 g) cauliflower
2 cups yoghurt
2 teaspoons ground ginger
2 teaspoons chopped coriander leaves
2 teaspoons sugar
salt to taste
½ cup oil *or* butter
2 onions, sliced
¼ cup raisins
½ cup green peas
6 red chillies, chopped
1 teaspoon *garam masala*

Cut cauliflower into bite-sized pieces. Wash and leave them on a tea towel to dry.

Put yoghurt in a bowl. Add ginger, chopped coriander leaves, sugar and salt. Mix well. Marinate cauliflower in this mixture for 2 hours.

Heat oil or butter in a pan over medium heat and brown onions. Add raisins, peas, cauliflower mixture, ½ cup hot water, chopped chillies and *garam masala*. Stir well, cover pan and simmer on low heat till cauliflower is tender and liquid has been absorbed. Serve with bread and *chapati* or rice.

Cauliflower in Cheese

Oven setting ' 150°C, 300°F, Gas Regulo 4
Serves   : 8

3 pounds (1350 g) cauliflower
2 teaspoons chopped ginger
salt to taste
2 cups coconut milk from ½ pound (225 g) grated coconut
1 teaspoon black pepper, crushed
6 green chillies, chopped
½ cup roasted cashew-nuts, ground
12 shallots, peeled and left whole
¼ cup melted ghee *or* oil
½ cup grated cheese
2 teaspoons chopped coriander leaves
4 tomatoes, sliced

Cut cauliflower into bite-sized pieces, wash and leave on a tea towel to dry.

Place cauliflower, ginger, and salt in a saucepan. Add coconut milk and black pepper. Boil the cauliflower mixture until it is dry and half-cooked.

Stir in chilli, ground cashew-nut, shallots and ghee. Remove from heat and pour into a casserole. Cover with grated cheese and bake in a moderately hot oven till brown.

Garnish with chopped coriander leaves and tomatoes. Serve with bread or *chapati*.

Baked Cauliflower Dom

Baking : *10 mins*
Oven setting: *150°C, 300°F, Gas Regulo 4*
Serves : *8*

3 pounds (1350 g) cauliflower (whole)
1 cup yoghurt, beaten
salt to taste
2 teaspoons sugar
1 tablespoon ground onion
1 tablespoon ground ginger
3 tablespoons ground cashew-nuts
1 tablespoon ground raisins
1 tablespoon ground green chillies
1 teaspoon *garam masala*
a few tomato slices and some green peas for
   garnishing
½ cup butter oil

Remove the main stem from the base of the cauliflower. Make small cuts at the base to ensure even cooking but leave the cauliflower whole. Wash and place cauliflower with yoghurt, salt, sugar and 1 cup water in a heavy saucepan. Cover tightly and simmer over medium heat until the cauliflower is almost cooked.

Heat butter oil in a pan and add ground ingredients, *garam masala* and a little water. Fry for a few minutes.

Put cauliflower in its sauce in a casserole and pour the fried ingredients over it. Bake in a moderately hot oven for 10 minutes. Turn the cauliflower over carefully, spoon some of the liquid in the casserole over it and continue baking till light brown. Remove from the oven and garnish with sliced tomatoes and peas before serving. Serve with *paratha* or bread.

Vegetable in Cream (Navaratnam Curry)

Serves: 10

1 pound (450 g) cauliflower
1 small beetroot
a few cabbage leaves
2 carrots
½ pound (225 g) French beans
salt to taste
½ pound (225 g) new potatoes
½ cup butter oil
2 teaspoons chopped ginger
2 onions, sliced
3-4 red chillies, chopped
1 teaspoon crushed black pepper
1 cup cream, beaten
½ cup tomato puree
1 cup yoghurt
½ pound (225 g) green peas
1 teaspoon sugar
1 teaspoon lemon juice

Cut cauliflower, beetroot, cabbage and carrots into small pieces and the French beans into 2-4 diagonal sections, depending on the size. Boil with a little salt till half-cooked, then drain.

Scrub and cut new potatoes into half, leaving very small ones whole. Fry in butter till light brown. Remove to a dish. In the same oil, lightly brown ginger and onions before adding the boiled vegetables, fried potatoes, chillies and black pepper. Fry for a further 10 minutes.

Mix cream with tomato puree and yoghurt. Add this to the vegetable mixture, followed by green peas, sugar and salt. Stir to mix, then cover the pan and simmer till all vegetables are cooked. Add lemon juice. (Some steamed prawns may be added, if desired.)

Serve with bread or rice.

Masoor Dhal

Serves: 6

1 pound (450 g) *masoor dhal*
salt to taste
2 teaspoons ground turmeric
3-4 green chillies, coarsely sliced
¼ cup ghee *or* **oil**
3-4 dried chillies, cut into 2 or 3 sections
1 teaspoon fenugreek
2 onions, chopped

Wash *dhal* well and boil in 6 cups water with salt and ground turmeric. When *dhal* is well cooked (the grains should be soft and somewhat broken and the mixture should give a thick consistency), add fresh green chillies and sugar and remove from heat.

Heat ghee in a saucepan and fry dried chillies, fenugreek and onions for a few minutes. Pour in boiled *dhal* and cook for a few minutes before removing from heat to get a "soupy" *dhal.*

Serve with bread, *chapati* or plain rice.

Channa Dhal

Serves: 6

½ pound (225 g) *channa dhal*
salt to taste
1 teaspoon ground turmeric
2 tablespoons ghee
3 dried chillies, cut into 2 or 3 sections
1 teaspoon cummin
2-3 bay leaves
2 teaspoons chopped ginger
2 onions, chopped
1 tablespoon finely chopped coconut
1 teaspoon *garam masala*
2-3 green chillies, coarsely sliced
1 teaspoon sugar

Soak *dhal* for about 1 hour, then wash and boil with salt and ground turmeric in 4 cups water. When *dhal* is soft and cooked, remove from heat.

Heat ghee in a saucepan and fry dried chillies, cummin, bay leaves, ginger, onions and coconut till brown. Add *garam masala* and fry for a futher 2-3 minutes. Add cooked *dhal,* green chillies and sugar. Boil for a few more minutes before removing from heat. Serve with bread, *chapati* or *loochi.*

Stuffed Cabbage

Baking : *20 mins*
Oven setting: *205 °C, 400 °F, Gas Regulo 8*
Serves : *6*

1 cabbage
salt to taste
2 tablespoons ghee *or* oil
½ pound (225 g) minced mutton
1 tablespoon tomato puree
2 eggs, beatèn
2 carrots, diced
2 tablespoons green peas
3 onions, chopped
4 cloves garlic, chopped
1 teaspoon roasted ground cummin
2 teaspoons ground chilli
1 teaspoon ginger juice
2 teaspoons chopped coriander leaves
1 teaspoon sugar
extra ghee *or* butter for baking
red chillies for garnishing

Boil a large pot of water sufficient to cover the cabbage. Put in the whole cabbage, add salt and simmer till three-quarters cooked. Drain off water and set aside to cool. When cool, carefully part the cabbage leaves one by one. Remove the central stump and make a hollow.

Heat ghee in a pan and fry minced mutton and all other ingredients for a few minutes. Add 2 cups water, cover pan and cook till meat is tender and all moisture absorbed.

Stuff the cabbage with curried mutton and rub the leaves inside with a little tomato puree. Use toothpicks to close the opening.

Place the cabbage on a greased baking tray, brush with a little ghee or butter and cover. Bake for about 20 minutes in a moderately hot oven. Garnish with red chillies and serve with any sauce.

Cabbage Roll Bhaji

Serves: 6

12 cabbage leaves
1 pound (450 g) shrimps
oil *or* ghee for deep-fat frying
5 cloves garlic, chopped
3 onions, chopped
2 teaspoons chopped ginger
1 tablespoon ground chilli
1 teaspoon *garam masala*
salt to taste
1 teaspoon sugar
1 teaspoon roasted ground cummin
4 eggs, beaten
1 cup *channa dhal* flour
½ cup rice flour
2 tablespoons tomato puree
some toothpicks

Boil cabbage leaves in salt water till half-cooked, then drain well. Clean and shell shrimps, boil, then pound.

Heat 2 tablespoons oil or ghee in a pan over medium heat and fry garlic, onions and ginger for a few minutes. Add pounded shrimps, ground chilli, *garam masala*, salt, sugar, ground cummin, 3 beaten eggs and ½ cup water. Fry till dry and remove from heat.

In a bowl, mix *dhal* and rice flour, ½ teaspoon salt, 1 beaten egg and sufficient water to make a soft batter.

Take one cabbage leaf, spread a little tomato puree on it, then put in a little of the prawn mixture and roll up. Secure with 2 toothpicks.

Do this till there is neither prawn mixture nor cabbage leaf left. Dip the rolls into batter and deep-fry till brown. Drain well before serving with sauce or salad.

Doh Piaji (Stuffed Onions)

Baking   : *20 mins*
Oven setting : *205°C, 400°F, Gas Regulo 8*
Makes   : *20*

20 big onions
1 tablespoon ghee *or* oil
1 pound (450 g) minced mutton
6 cloves garlic, chopped
2 onions, chopped
2 teaspoons ginger juice
3 teaspoons ground chilli
2 teaspoons roasted ground cummin
1 teaspoon *garam masala*
2 teaspoons chopped coriander leaves
1 teaspoon sugar
salt to taste
1 pound (450 g) prawns, shelled
2 eggs, beaten
1 tablespoon plain white flour

Peel the 20 large onions and slice off about ¼ inch (½ cm) from the top. Using a small sharp knife, cut away the centre of each onion to make a hole as wide and as deep as possible.

Heat 1 tablespoon ghee in a pan and fry mutton with all ingredients except prawns, flour and beaten eggs. Add a little water. Cover and simmer till mutton is tender and moisture absorbed. Add prawns, beaten eggs, stirring rapidly to mix. When all ingredients are cooked, remove from heat and set aside for a few minutes to cool a little.

Stuff onions with the mutton mixture. Mix flour with a little water to make a paste. Cover the opening of each onion with a little paste and bake in a moderately hot oven for 20 minutes or deep-fry in oil till brown. Serve with *chutney.*

Note: Tomatoes and potatoes may be substituted for onions.

Eggplant Kalia

Serves: 8

2 pounds (900 g) eggplants
2 teaspoons salt
4 teaspoons ground turmeric
2 tablespoons ghee *or* oil
½ teaspoon sweet cummin
4 cloves garlic, chopped
3 onions, sliced
2 teaspoons chopped ginger
3 teaspoons ground chilli
1 teaspoon sugar
1 cup yoghurt
1 tablespoon tomato puree
2 teaspoons chopped coriander leaves
2 teaspoons roasted ground sweet cummin
salt to taste

Cut eggplants lengthwise into 2 pieces, wash and rub with 2 teaspoons salt and 2 teaspoons ground turmeric.

Heat ghee *or* oil in a pan over medium heat and fry sweet cummin, garlic, onions and ginger till lightly browned. Add eggplants and fry for about 8 minutes. Add 1 cup water, ground turmeric, ground chilli and sugar and fry for a few more minutes before adding yoghurt and tomato puree. Simmer till liquid has dried up, then add chopped coriander leaves and roasted ground sweet cummin. Toss to mix and remove from heat. Serve with rice or bread.

Vegetable Dhal

Serves: 6

1 pound (450 g) *moong dhal* **(green split beans).**
4 cups water
2 teaspoons ground turmeric
1 teaspoon salt
4 potatoes
2 carrots
¼ pound (110 g) cauliflower
4 tablespoons ghee *or* **oil**
1 teaspoon sugar
a few French beans, cut into 2 or 3 sections
a few cabbage leaves, cut into small pieces
2 radishes, cut into small pieces
3 tomatoes, halved
2 tablespoons green peas
3-4 green chillies, sliced
2 teaspoons chopped coriander leaves
4 dried chillies
½ teaspoon cummin
2 sticks cinnamon
4 pods cardamom
3 bay leaves
3 teaspoons ginger, chopped
4 onions, sliced
1 teaspoon *garam masala*

Fry *dhal* in a clean dry pan over low heat till slightly browned. Wash and boil with 4 cups water, ground turmeric and 1 teaspoon salt in a covered pan.

Scrape potatoes and carrots. Cut these and cauliflower into large sections. Heat 1 tablespoon ghee and stir-fry potatoes, carrots and cauliflower till potatoes are light brown, then remove to a dish.

When *dhal* is three-quarters cooked (after about 30 minutes), add sugar, French beans, cabbage and radishes. When vegetables are tender, add tomatoes, peas, green chillies and coriander leaves and remove *dhal* from heat.

Heat 1 tablespoon ghee in a *wok* over medium heat and fry dried chillies, cummin, cinnamon and cardamom for a minute, then add bay leaves, ginger and onions. Stir-fry for about 10 minutes, then pour *dhal,* vegetables and green peas into the *wok* and allow to simmer for 10 minutes. Add *garam masala* and remove from heat.

Serve with rice or *chapati.*

Bhindi Curry

Serves: 6

1 pound (450 g) *moong dhal* **(green split beans).**
1 pound (450 g) young okra *or vindi* **(lady's fingers)**
salt to taste
½ cup oil
1 teaspoon fenugreek
2 onions, sliced
1 teaspoon ground turmeric
2 teaspoons ground chilli
½ cup yoghurt or tomato puree
1 teaspoon sugar
2-3 red chillies, sliced

Wash and cut okra into two, rub with a little salt and set aside.

Heat oil in a pan over medium heat and fry fenugreek and onions for a few minutes. Add okra, ground turmeric and chilli, yoghurt (or tomato puree), sugar and salt. Cover the pan and cook on low heat, stirring occasionally. When vegetable is tender and curry almost dry, add sliced red chillies and remove from heat.

Note: Some shrimps may be added if desired.

Matar Panir

Serves: 10

4 cups milk
2 tablespoons lemon juice
½ pound (225 g) potatoes
½ teaspoon cummin seeds
2 tablespoons melted ghee *or* butter
½ tablespoon ground chilli
2 teaspoons ground cummin
1 teaspoon ground turmeric
2-3 bay leaves
1 teaspoon sugar
salt to taste
½ cup yoghurt
½ cup green peas
1 teaspoon *garam masala*
3 tomatoes, sliced

To make panir

Heat 4 cups milk in a saucepan, stirring continuously to prevent a skim from forming on top. As soon as it comes to a boil, add lemon juice and remove from heat. Stir slowly till milk has completely curdled.

Strain through a muslin cloth. The residue, called *channa,* is hung up to drip in the muslin, then wrapped around in the cloth and compressed by some heavy weights (any flat object weighing about 5 pounds) to obtain *panir,* a soft cheese, after a few hours. Cut the slab of cheese into cubes and keep refrigerated till required.

To make matar panir

Halve the potatoes, then cut each half into ½ inch (1 cm) slices.

Heat the oil in a pan over medium heat and lightly brown the panir pieces. Remove to a dish. In the same oil, fry cummin seeds for a minute, then add potatoes and fry till brown. Pour in ½ cup water and add ground chilli, cummin and turmeric, bay leaves, sugar, salt and yoghurt. Fry for about 5 minutes, then add 3 cups water and panir. Boil till potatoes are cooked and there is just a little gravy left. Add *garam masala,* peas and sliced tomatoes, season to taste and remove from heat after another 2-3 minutes. Serve with bread or rice.

Potato Dom

Serves: 6

1 pound (450 g) small potatoes
2-3 bay leaves
½ teaspoon cummin
2 teaspoons ground turmeric
1 teaspoons ground chilli
2 teaspoons ginger juice
1 teaspoon sugar
juice from 2 onions
½ cup yoghurt
2 teaspoons melted butter
1 teaspoon *garam masala*
2 tomatoes, sliced
salt to taste
½ cup oil

Peel potatoes. Halve big ones and leave small ones whole. Deep-fry in ½ cup oil till brown. Remove to a dish.

In the same oil, fry bay leaves and cummin seeds for a minute, then add turmeric and chilli, ginger juice, sugar, onion juice and yoghurt. Fry for 5 minutes till raw smell goes off, then add potatoes and ½ cup water. When potatoes are cooked and gravy is thick, stir in 2 teaspoons roasted cummin, melted butter, *garam masala* and sliced tomatoes. Remove from heat at once and serve with plain rice, *chapati* or *loochi.*

Labra (Mixed Vegetables)

Serves : 10

2 sweet potatoes
2 potatoes
¼ pound (110 g) pumpkin
¼ pound (110 g) cabbage
2 eggplants
¼ pound (110 g) French beans
2 radishes
½ cup ghee *or* oil
3-4 dried chillies
2 teaspoons panch masala
2 teaspoons ground turmeric
1 teaspoon ground chilli
1 teaspoon sugar
salt to taste
3-4 red chillies, sliced
2-3 teaspoons chopped coriander leaves
2 teaspoons flour

Peel sweet potatoes, potatoes and pumpkin. Cut sweet potatoes, potatoes, cabbage and eggplants into 2 inch (5 cm) pieces. String French beans and halve them. Scrape radishes and cut into 2 inch (5 cm) pieces. Wash and dry all vegetables.

Heat three-quarters of ghee in a pan over medium heat and fry dried chillies and *panch masala* till the dried chillies are puffed up. Put in the vegetables and stir for 5 minutes before adding ground turmeric, ground chilli, sugar and salt to taste. Cover the pan and simmer till vegetables are tender and cooked.

Add sliced red chillies and chopped coriander leaves to the vegetables when they are cooked. Add a little water to the flour to make a paste and thicken the gravy with this paste before removing from heat.

Serve with bread or rice.

Cutlets

Vegetable Cutlet

Makes : 25

1 pound (450 g) *channa dhal*
1 ¼ pounds (560 g) potatoes
¼ pound (110 g) cauliflower
¼ pound (110 g) carrots
¼ pound (110 g) cabbage
2 tablespoons green peas
2 onions, chopped
2 teaspoons chopped ginger
1 teaspoon sugar
5 teaspoons ground chilli
salt to taste
1 teaspoon roasted ground cummin
2 teaspoons *garam masala*
1 tablespoon plain white flour
breadcrumbs
2 eggs, beaten
2 cups ghee *or* oil

Soak *channa dhal* for 1 hour, then wash and boil with ½ teaspoon salt and 4 cups water till soft and dry. Boil 1 pound (450 g) potatoes in their jackets. When cool, peel off the remaining ¼ pound (110 g) of potatoes and scrape carrots. Cut potatoes, cauliflower, carrots and cabbage into very small pieces.

Heat 2 tablespoons ghee and fry chopped onions and ginger for a few minutes. Then add cut potatoes, cauliflower, carrots, cabbage and green peas, with sugar, 3 teaspoons ground chilli and salt to taste. Fry for a few minutes till vegetables are well coated with ghee, then add ½ cup water and cover the pan. Continue cooking on low heat till vegetables are tender. Stir in roasted ground cummin and 1 teaspoon *garam masala* and remove from heat.

Put potatoes, *channa dhal,* flour, 2 teaspoons ground chilli, 1 teaspoon *garam masala* and 1 teaspoon salt into a mixing bowl and knead well. Shape a lump of this mixture, the size of a "ping pong" ball, into a cup, place some vegetable curry into the hollow, draw in the rim of the cup and pat into flat round shapes.

Coat with breadcrumbs, dip into beaten egg and coat with breadcrumbs once again. Heat the remaining ghee or oil in a pan over low heat and deep-fry the cutlets till golden brown. Drain well and serve with chilli sauce and *chutney.*

Mutton Rib Cutlet

Makes : 12

12 mutton rib sections, about 3 inches (7½ cm)
  long
2 slices bread
½ cup milk
4 onions, sliced
ghee *or* oil for deep-fat frying
1 teaspoon chopped garlic
1 teaspoon ground cinnamon
1 teaspoon ground cardamom
1 pound (450 g) minced mutton
4 eggs, beaten
2 teaspoons ground chilli
2 teaspoons ginger juice
1 teaspoon sugar
salt to taste
2 teaspoons chopped coriander leaves
1 teaspoon roasted ground cummin
1 tablespoon plain white flour
breadcrumbs

Boil the mutton rib sections. Soak bread slices in milk. Fry half the sliced onions in 2 tablespoons oil or ghee and remove to a dish.

In the same oil, fry garlic, ground cinnamon, cardamom and the rest of the sliced onions till slightly brown. Then stir in minced mutton, 2 beaten eggs, ground chilli, ginger juice, sugar and salt. Fry for a few minutes to release meat juices, then add ½ cup water and continue cooking on low heat till mutton is quite dry and tender.

Mix fried mutton with fried onions, soaked bread, chopped coriander leaves, roasted ground cummin, white flour and a little more salt. Knead well till mixture is smooth and no lumps remain. Divide the mixture into 12 equal portions and shape into flat rectangular cakes of about 2 inch (5 cm) width. Place a rib section in the centre and roll the cake around it.

Coat the cutlets in breadcrumbs, dip in beaten egg and roll in breadcrumbs once again before deep-frying till dark brown. Serve with chilli sauce, *chutney* and salad.

Cheese Cutlet

Makes : 12

2 pounds (900 g) potatoes
½ pound (225 g) grated Cheddar or Parmesan
  cheese
10 ounces (300 g) onions, finely chopped
1 egg, beaten
1 cup rice flour
3-4 green chillies, chopped
2 teaspoons chopped coriander leaves
1 teaspoon ground chilli
2 teaspoons roasted ground cummin
1 teaspoon baking powder
2 teaspoons sugar
salt to taste
ghee *or* oil for deep-fat frying

Boil potatoes in their jackets, then peel and mash well. Mix mashed potatoes with all the ingredients except ghee. Knead well for at least 5 minutes.

Divide the mixture into small lumps slightly bigger than walnuts and pat into round, flat shapes. Heat the ghee or oil in a *wok* and fry a few cutlets at a time till deep golden. Drain well and serve with chilli sauce.

Fish Cutlet

Makes : 6

1 pound (450 g) threadfin (*ikan kurau*) fillet
2 tablespoons yoghurt
2 teaspoons ground turmeric
2 teaspoons ground chilli
2 teaspoons ginger juice
1 onion, ground
1 teaspoon sugar
salt to taste
2 eggs, beaten
2 tablespoons ground *channa dhal*
2 teaspoons lemon juice
breadcrumbs
ghee *or* oil for deep-fat frying

Cut fish into long, flat pieces, wash and dry them. Rub with yoghurt, ground turmeric, chilli, ginger juice, ground onion, sugar and salt. Set aside to marinate for 4 hours, then pound lightly to flatten.

Mix beaten eggs with ground *dhal,* lemon juice and a little salt. Beat with a fork to mix well. Dip fish pieces into this mixture, then coat with breadcrumbs. Deep-fry a few pieces at a time till golden brown. Drain well and serve hot with salad.

Cauliflower Cutlet

Makes : 16

2 pounds (900 g) cauliflower
ghee *or* oil for deep-fat frying
3 teaspoons ground chilli
1 teaspoon *garam masala*
2 teaspoons ginger juice
1 teaspoon sugar
salt to taste
1 teaspoon roasted ground cummin
¼ cup green peas
3 pounds (1350 g) potatoes
1 tablespoon plain white flour
1 teaspoon pepper
breadcrumbs
2 eggs, beaten

When tender, add ground cummin and green peas and remove from heat after 5 minutes.

Boil and peel potatoes. When cool, mash with flour, pepper and salt. Divide mashed potatoes into 16 equal portions. Make a hollow in the centre of each and fill with cauliflower. Close hollows and pat into flat round cakes. Coat the cakes with bread-crumbs, dip in beaten egg, then coat with breadcrumbs again before deep-fat frying, 2 or 3 at a time, to a golden brown.

Cut cauliflower into very small pieces. Fry in 2 tablespoons oil with ground chilli, *garam masala,* ginger juice, sugar and salt.

Note: Substitutes for cauliflower — cabbage, white radish, carrots.

Egg Cutlet

Makes : 16

4 hardboiled eggs
1 pound (450 g) potatoes
ghee *or* oil for deep-fat frying
1 tablespoon plain white flour
2 teaspoons black pepper
2 eggs, beaten
2 teaspoons finely chopped ginger
2 onions, chopped
¼ cup green peas
2 teaspoons ground chilli
1 teaspoon *garam masala*
1 teaspoon roasted ground cummin
2 teaspoons chopped coriander leaves
1 teaspoon sugar
salt to taste
breadcrumbs

Mash hardboiled eggs and set aside. Boil potatoes, then peel and mash. Heat 1 tablespoon ghee or oil in a pan and fry mashed potato with flour, black pepper and a little salt for a few minutes. Spread to cool.

Heat 1 tablespoon ghee in a pan over medium heat and fry ginger and onions for 2-3 minutes. Add mashed eggs, green peas, ground chilli, *garam masala,* ground cummin, chopped coriander leaves, sugar and salt to taste. Fry till peas are tender and no liquid remains, and remove from heat.

Divide mashed potato mixture into 16 equal portions. Shape into cups, put some egg mixture into each hollow, then draw in the rims and pat into flat, round shapes. Coat with breadcrumbs, dip into beaten egg, then coat with breadcrumbs again before deep-drying in ghee or oil till brown. Serve with any sauce.

Mutton Cutlet

Makes : 20

2 pounds (900 g) potatoes
1 tablespoon plain white flour
2 teaspoons black pepper
salt to taste
ghee *or* oil for deep-fat frying
5 cloves garlic, chopped
6 onions, sliced
2 green chillies, chopped
1 pound (450 g) minced mutton
1 teaspoon ground chilli
1 teaspoon ginger juice
1 teaspoon sugar
2 teaspoons chopped coriander leaves
1 teaspoon *garam masala*
2 teaspoons roasted ground cummin
2 eggs, beaten
breadcrumbs

Boil potatoes till tender, then peel and mash them. Mix with flour, black pepper, salt to taste and 2 teaspoons ghee.

Heat 1 tablespoon ghee in a pan and fry garlic, onions and green chillies for a few minutes. Then add mutton, ground chilli, ginger juice, sugar and salt and fry for a few more minutes. Add ½ cup water, cover the pan and simmer till mutton is dry and tender, then add chopped coriander leaves, *garam masala* and roasted ground cummin. Fry for 2-3 minutes more, then remove from heat.

Shape a lump of mashed potato into a cup, put some mutton into the hollow and draw in the rim of the cup. Pat into a flat shape. Dip into beaten egg and coat with breadcrumbs.

Heat ghee or oil for deep-fat frying and fry a few cutlets at a time till golden brown. Drain well and serve with salad and *chutney.*

Eggs

Egg and Meat Malad

Baking : *20 mins.*
Oven setting : *150°C, 300°F, Gas Regulo 4*
Serves : *8*

1 pound (450 g) finely minced mutton
½ teaspoon sugar
salt to taste
2 teaspoons vinegar
2 teaspoons ginger juice
½ cup yoghurt
2 tablespoons ghee *or* oil
5 cloves garlic, chopped
3 onions, finely chopped
1 tablespoon ground chilli
2 teaspoons chopped coriander leaves
1 tablespoon tomato puree
1 tablespoon cornflour
4 eggs, beaten
1 teaspoon black pepper
2 tablespoons breadcrumbs

Marinate minced mutton in sugar, salt, vinegar, ginger juice and yoghurt for 2 hours.

Heat 1 tablespoon oil in a pan over medium heat and fry garlic and onions for 10 minutes, then add meat, ground chilli and chopped coriander leaves. Fry till liquid has dried up. Add 1 cup cold water, stir to mix. Then cover the pan and boil till mutton is cooked. Stir in tomato puree and a cornflour paste made by mixing 1 tablespoon cornflour with 1 tablespoon water. When gravy has dried up, remove the pan from heat.

Mix beaten eggs with pepper and salt. Grease a baking tin and spread half the breadcrumbs in it. On top of this, spread half the mutton. Coat the top with half the egg mixture, then spread the remaining mutton over this. Cover with the rest of the egg and sprinkle liberally with breadcrumbs. Bake for 20 minutes in a moderately hot oven till light brown. Cut into squares and serve with salad.

Egg Pillau

Serves : 10

2 pounds (900 g) *Patna* rice
1 teaspoon ground turmeric
2 teaspoons ground cummin
2 teaspoons ground chilli
2 teaspoons ground onion
1 teaspoon sugar
salt to taste
1 coconut, grated
5 hardboiled eggs
2 tablespoons thin milk
1 tablespoon plain white flour
½ cup ghee *or* oil
2-3 sticks cinnamon
2 onions, sliced
2 teaspoons ground ginger

Wash rice. Drain well in a sieve for 10 minutes. Mix rice with ground turmeric, cummin and chilli, 1 teaspoon ground onion, sugar and salt. Set aside. Extract 2 cups coconut milk from grated coconut.

Halve the hardboiled eggs. Make a batter with thin milk, flour, remaining ground onion and salt. Dip egg halves in this batter and fry in oil or ghee till the whites are light brown. Remove to a dish.

In the same oil, fry cinnamon, cardamom and sliced onions for 4-5 minutes. Add the rice mixture, ground ginger and salt, and fry till rice is light brown. Add coconut milk and enough water to bring the liquid level to 2 inches (5 cm) above the rice.

Boil over medium heat, stirring frequently till all the liquid is absorbed. Make a few hollows in the rice, put in the fried egg halves and push rice over the eggs. Cover pan and finish cooking over very low heat, Serve with curry or *chutney.*

Egg Omelette Curry

Serves : 6

4 eggs, beaten
1 tablespoon thin milk
1 onion, sliced
salt to taste
½ cup oil
½ pound (225 g) potatoes
1 stick cinnamon
2-3 pods cardamom
½ teaspoon cummin
1 onion, ground
3 cloves garlic, ground
2 teaspoons ground turmeric
2 teaspoons ground cummin
2 teaspoons ground chilli
½ teaspoon sugar
2 tomatoes, sliced
3 red chillies, sliced
2 tablespoons cooked green peas

Mix beaten eggs with milk, onion slices and salt. Heat half the oil in a frying pan and fry egg mixture. When cooked, remove to a board and roll it. Cut omelette into 2 inch (5 cm) rolls.

Peel and quarter potatoes. Fry in remaining oil till slightly browned. Remove to a dish. In the same oil, fry cinnamon, cardamoms and cummin seeds for 1 minute, then add ground onion and garlic. Fry for 1-2 minutes till fragrant, then add ground turmeric, ground cummin, ground chilli, sugar and sliced tomatoes. After 2-3 minutes, add ¼ cup water and salt. Stir mixture continuously.

When the liquid dries up, add fried potatoes and 1½ cups water. Boil till potatoes are tender, then stir in egg rolls, chillies and cooked green peas. Remove from heat at once and serve with rice or bread.

Egg Dhoka

Serves : 8

6 eggs, beaten
1 onion, finely chopped
4 teaspoons ground chilli
½ pound (225 g) potatoes, sliced
1 teaspoon cummin
2 onions, ground
4 cloves garlic, ground
2 teaspoons ginger juice
2 teaspoons ground cummin
2 teaspoons ground turmeric
1 teaspoon sugar
1 tomato, sliced
1 teaspoon *garam masala*
salt to taste
¼ cup ghee *or* oil

Mix beaten eggs with chopped onion, 1 teaspoon ground chilli and salt. Rub the inside of a heatproof bowl with a little ghee or oil. Put the egg mixture into the bowl and steam till it hardens. Remove the bowl and allow it to cool in a pan of cold water, then take out the egg pudding and cut into pieces. Peel and cut potatoes into ½ inch (1 cm) slices.

Heat oil or ghee in a pan over medium heat and fry egg pieces till lightly browned. Remove to a dish. In the same oil, fry potato slices till golden. Remove slices to a dish.

Again using the same oil, fry cummin seeds for 1 minute, then add ground onions, garlic and ginger juice. Fry for at least 5 minutes, stirring all the while, before adding ground cummin, ground turmeric, the remaining ground chilli and sugar. After 2-3 minutes, add fried potato slices and egg pieces. Stir carefully to avoid breaking the egg pieces. Add 2 cups water and simmer till potato slices are tender. Add tomato slices and *garam masala* when only a little gravy remains. Remove from heat after 1-2 minutes. Serve with bread or rice.

Egg Devil

Serves : 6

8 eggs
4 large potatoes
ghee *or* oil for deep-fat frying
1 pound (450 g) finely minced mutton
1 tablespoon ground chilli
4 cloves garlic, chopped
2 teaspoons ground ginger
4 onions, thinly sliced
1 teaspoon sugar
salt to taste
2 teaspoons roasted ground cummin
1 teaspoon *garam masala*
2 teaspoons chopped coriander leaves
1 tablespoon plain white flour
1 teaspoon black pepper
2 eggs, beaten
breadcrumbs

Boil eggs and potatoes together. When cooked, remove from heat and cool in a pan of cold water. Shell eggs, make a slit along one side and remove yolks.

Heat 2 tablespoons oil or ghee in a frying pan and fry mutton with ground chilli, garlic, ginger, onions, sugar and salt. Add ¼ cup water, if necessary. When mutton is cooked and dry, remove from the pan and grind or pound well. Mix with ground cummin, *garam masala* and chopped coriander leaves.

Mix half the ground mutton with mashed egg yolks and stuff each egg white case with this mixture. Peel and mash potatoes with flour, pepper, salt and remaining mutton to make a paste. Cover each stuffed egg with a layer of this paste. Dip into beaten egg, coat with breadcrumbs and deep-fry over medium heat till brown. Serve with salad and *chutney*.

Egg Doh Piazi

Serves : 8

6 hardboiled eggs
2 eggs, beaten
2 teaspoons plain white flour
1 teaspoon ginger juice
salt to taste
½ cup oil *or* ghee
2 onions, ground
2 teaspoons ground chilli
1 teaspoon ground turmeric
1 teaspoon sugar
½ cup yoghurt
2 tablespoons cooked green peas
1 teaspoon *garam masala*
2-3 bay leaves

Shell the eggs and cut lengthwise into 4 pieces. Mix beaten eggs with a paste of flour, ginger juice, 2 teaspoons water and salt. Dip egg quarters into this batter and fry in ghee or oil over medium heat till golden brown. Remove to a dish.

Strain the oil and reheat in a clean pan. Fry sliced onions till golden brown and remove to a dish. In the same oil, fry ground onions till fragrant, then add ground chilli, ground turmeric, sugar, salt and yoghurt. Stir-fry for 5 minutes before adding ½ cup water and fried eggs. Cook till gravy thickens, then add green peas, *garam masala,* fried onions and bay leaves. Mix well and remove from heat. Serve with bread or rice.

Egg Roll

Oven setting : 300°F, 100°C, Gas Regulo 4
Makes   : 4

2 eggs, beaten
1 pound (450 g) finely minced mutton
2 teaspoons chopped ginger
3 green chillies, finely chopped
2 onions, finely chopped
1 teaspoon chopped garlic
1 teaspoon sugar
1 teaspoon black pepper
2 teaspoons chopped coriander leaves
1 teaspoon *garam masala*
1 teaspoon roasted ground cummin
salt to taste
3 tablespoons ghee *or* oil

Batter

6 eggs, beaten
½ cup self-raising flour
½ cup *channa dhal* flour
1 teaspoon baking powder
½ cup unsweetened milk
juice from 1 onion
1 teaspoon sugar
1 teaspoon salt

Heat 1 tablespoon ghee or oil over medium heat and fry ginger, green chillies, onions and garlic till slightly brown. Add minced mutton, sugar, salt and pepper and fry for 5-10 minutes. Add ¼ cup water, cover the pan and simmer till mutton is cooked. Stir in 2 beaten eggs, chopped coriander leaves, *garam masala* and roasted ground cummin. Cook till dry and remove from heat.

Mix all the batter ingredients and beat well till smooth. Add a little water if necessary. Heat a frying pan over low heat and, using a small cloth, rub a little ghee or oil on its surface. Put 1 tablespoon of the batter into the pan and spread with the bottom of the spoon. When the pancake is cooked, remove to a flat dish, spread with cooked mutton and roll carefully.

Arrange the rolls on a baking tray and bake in a slow oven to make them crisp. Serve at teatime with chilli or tomato sauce and a salad.

Seafood

Tandoori Fish

Baking   : 20 mins.
Oven setting : 205°C, 400°F, Gas Regulo 8
Serves   : 6

2 pounds (900 g) fish fillet
1 teaspoon salt
1 teaspoon lemon juice
2 cloves garlic
2½ cm (1 in) piece ginger
4 dried chillies
1 teaspoon *garam masala*
½ cup yoghurt
1 drop yellow colouring
3 tablespoons melted butter
2 tomatoes, sliced into rings
1 lemon, sliced

Make deep cuts on both sides of fish.

Rub with salt and lemon juice. Set aside for 20 minutes.

Grind garlic, ginger and dried chillies together till a smooth paste is obtained. Mix ground ingredients with *garam masala*, yoghurt and yellow colouring.

Place fish in a baking tray and pour mixture over it. Keep at room temperature for 4 hours, after which, set oven and bake fish for 20 minutes till light brown. When fish is three-quarters done, brush melted butter over it.

Serve garnished with lemons and tomato slices.

Fish Dom Pokto

Baking   : 20 mins.
Oven setting : 105°C, 300°F, Gas Regulo 4
Serves   : 8

2 pounds (900 g) threadfin (ikan kurau)
juice from 2 onions
2 teaspoons ginger juice
½ cup beaten yoghurt
1 teaspoon black peppercorns, crushed
8 almonds, ground
2 teaspoons raisins, ground
1 teaspoon ground turmeric
2-3 red chillies, finely sliced
2 tablespoons melted butter or oil
½ teaspoon sugar
salt to taste
8 whole tomatoes

Cut fish into pieces, wash and dry. Rub the pieces with salt and turmeric. Place in a casserole with a mixture of all the other ingredients and tomatoes. Cover and bake for 20 minutes in a moderately hot oven. Serve hot with bread or *pillau*.

Fish in Cream

Baking : 20 mins.
Oven setting : 205°C, 400°F, Gas Regulo 8
Serves : 4

1 pound (450 g) threadfin (*ikan kurau*) *or*
   mackerel (*ikan tenggiri*)
juice from 1 onion
2 teaspoons ginger juice
2 tablespoons melted butter
¼ cup yoghurt
¼ cup cream
1 tablespoon tomato puree
3 red chillies, chopped
2 teaspoons raisins
salt to taste
2 teaspoons lemon juice
1 tomato, sliced
2 teaspoons chopped coriander leaves

Cut fish into 6 pieces, wash and dry. Mix onion juice, ginger juice, butter, yoghurt, cream, tomato puree, chillies, raisins and salt. Place fish pieces and the mixture in a casserole and bake in a moderately hot oven for 20 minutes till fish is cooked.

When fish is done, remove casserole from the oven and sprinkle with lemon juice. Garnish with tomato slices and chopped coriander leaves and serve hot with rice or bread.

Fish Chaloon

Serves : 8

2 pounds (900 g) fillet of threadfin (*ikan kurau*)
salt to taste
2 teaspoons ground turmeric
4 eggplants
2 potatoes, scraped
2 white radishes, scraped
1 cup oil
1 teaspoon black cummin
2 teaspoons ground garlic
3 onions, sliced
2 teaspoons ground ginger
4 teaspoons ground chilli
3 red chillies, each cut into 2 or 3 sections
8 teaspoons chopped spring onion
2 teaspoons chopped coriander leaves
½ cup French beans

Cut fish into 2-inch (5 cm) pieces. Wash and dry thoroughly. Rub with salt and ground turmeric. Cut eggplants, potatoes and radishes into 2-inch (5 cm) pieces. Wash, dry them and set aside.

Heat oil in a pan over medium heat and fry fish pieces till light brown. Remove to a dish. In the same oil, fry black cummin for half a minute. Add garlic and onion slices and fry till brown, then add vegetables, ground ginger, ground chilli and salt. Stir-fry till vegetables are half-cooked. Add fried fish and 2 cups water. Cover the pan and simmer.

When vegetables are cooked, add red chillies, chopped spring onion and coriander leaves. Mix well and continue cooking till mixture is almost dry. Serve with rice.

Tomato Fish

Baking   : *20 mins.*
Oven setting : *205 °C, 400 °F, Gas Regulo 8*
Serves   : *8*

2 pounds (900 g) threadfin (*ikan kurau*)
2 teaspoons ground turmeric
8 tomatoes
2 onions
3 teaspoons ground mustard seed
2 teaspoons ground chilli
3 teaspoons chopped parsley
1 tablespoon warm melted butter *or* oil
3 red chillies, sliced
1 tablespoon grated Parmesan *or* Cheddar
   cheese
2 teaspoons lemon juice
salt to taste

Cut fish into small pieces. Wash and rub with salt and ground turmeric. Leave aside for 30 minutes. In the meantime, cut tomatoes and onions into ¼ inch (½ cm) rings.

Mix fish pieces with ground mustard, ground chilli, chopped parsley and warm butter or oil.

Arrange some tomato rings on a greased baking tray and place fish pieces on top of these. Cover with remaining tomato rings, onion rings, red chillies and grated cheese. Bake in a moderately hot oven for 20 minutes. When fish is done, remove from oven and sprinkle lemon juice over the pieces. Serve with rice or *chapati.*

Green Chilli Fish

Baking   : *20 mins.*
Oven setting : *205 °C, 400 °F, Gas Regulo 8*
Serves   : *8*

2 pounds (900 g) threadfin (*ikan kurau*)
salt to taste
1 teaspoon ground turmeric
1 tablespoon first coconut milk
2 teaspoons ground ginger
1 onion, ground
1 egg, beaten
1 teaspoon black pepper
2 tablespoons warm melted butter *or* oil
2 tomatoes
1 pound (450 g) green chillies
1 6-inch (15 cm) piece banana leaf
   (or aluminium foil)
2 teaspoons lemon juice

Clean and cut fish into pieces. Dry well. In a bowl, mix salt, ground turmeric, coconut milk, ground ginger, ground onion, beaten egg, black pepper and warm butter or oil.

Marinate fish pieces in this mixture for 30 minutes.

Cut tomatoes into ¼ inch (½ cm) thick rings. Remove the stems of green chillies and leave them whole. Cover the bottom of a casserole with half the green chillies, arrange the fish on top and pour in the marinade. Spread a layer of tomato rings and remaining green chillies over the fish and cover with the banana leaf. Grill or bake for 20 minutes in a moderately hot oven. When fish is cooked, sprinkle lemon juice and serve with rice.

Dried Fish Pahee

Serves : 6

1 pound (450 g) dried threadfin (*ikan kurau*)
1 cup oil
10 curry leaves
8 cloves garlic, sliced
3 onions, sliced
½ cup red gourd (*labu merah*) cubes
a few cabbage leaves
2 potatoes, scraped and quartered
2 eggplants, each cut into 6-8 pieces
10 French beans, each cut into 2 or 3 sections
1 tablespoon ground chilli
2 teaspoons ground turmeric
3 teaspoons ground coriander
2 red chillies, sliced
¼ cup first coconut milk
2 teaspoons chopped coriander leaves
4 teaspoons lemon juice
salt to taste
1 cup oil

Cut fish into small pieces, wash and boil in 4 cups water for 10 minutes. Drain well and dry with a clean tea towel.

Heat oil in a pan over medium heat and fry fish pieces till light brown. Remove to a dish. Throw curry leaves into the same hot oil, followed immediately by garlic and onion slices. When these are brown, add all vegetables and ground ingredients. Stir-fry to mix well and cover the pan.

When vegetables are half-cooked, add fried fish, red chillies, salt, coconut milk and 2 cups water. Simmer till gravy thickens, then add chopped coriander leaves and lemon juice. Remove from heat. Serve with rice.

Dried Fish Pickle

2 pounds (900 g) dried threadfin (*ikan kurau*)
1 cup olive oil
2 teaspoons vinegar
2 tablespoons tamarind juice
8 cloves garlic, finely chopped
8 red chillies, sliced
10 shallots, peeled and left whole
2 teaspoons ground cummin
4 teaspoons ground mustard seed
3 teaspoons ground candlenuts
salt to taste

Cut fish into small pieces. Wash and soak in water for 2 hours. Remove fish and dry thoroughly with a tea towel. Heat ½ cup olive oil and fry fish pieces till light brown. Remove to a dish to cool.

Mix 1 teaspoon vinegar with tamarind juice. Heat remaining oil and fry garlic, chillies, shallots, ground cummin, ground mustard, ground candlenuts and salt to taste. Coat fish in this mixture and leave for 4 hours.

After 4 hours, add remaining vinegar to the fish. Place all the ingredients in a large clean jar and cover tightly. The fish should be ready for serving after a fortnight. Occasionally, leave the jar in the sun. Serve with plain rice.

Baked Fish and Cheese

Oven setting : 150°C, 300°F, Gas Regulo 4
Serves   : 2

1 pound (450 g) threadfin (*ikan kurau*)
  or mackerel (*ikan tenggiri*)
salt to taste
3 big potatoes
4 green chillies, chopped
1 onion, chopped
1½ tablespoons butter
3 eggs, beaten
2 teaspoons soy sauce
2 teaspoons gelatin
1 teaspoon pepper
3 tablespoons grated cheese
3 teaspoons chopped parsley

Rub fish with salt and steam. When cooked, scrape off the flesh and mash well with a fork. Boil potatoes, peel and cut into round slices about ½ inch (1 cm) thick. Sprinkle a little salt over the slices and set aside.

Mix mashed fish with chopped green chillies, onion, butter, beaten eggs, soy sauce, gelatin and pepper. Season to taste.

Grease a baking tray and arrange half the quantity of potato slices on the bottom. Place fish mixture on this and spread grated cheese on top of the fish. Cover with another layer of potato slices. Bake in a moderately hot oven till potato slices are brown. Remove from heat and cut into squares. Garnish with chopped parsley and serve hot with bread or *paratha*.

Dry Chilli Fish

Serves : 8

2 pounds (900 g) fillet of threadfin (*ikan kurau*)
2 teaspoons ground turmeric
½ pound (225 g) dried chillies
1 onion, sliced
3 tomatoes, quartered
1 stalk lemon grass, sliced
2 teaspoons ground ginger
1 tablespoon soy sauce
1 teaspoon sugar
2 tablespoons first coconut milk
2 teaspoons lemon juice
salt to taste
½ cup oil

Cut fish into small pieces, wash and drain well. Rub in ground turmeric and salt. Set aside.

Heat oil in a pan over medium heat. Fry dried chillies till puffy and dark brown. Remove to a dish. In the same oil, fry fish pieces till light brown. Remove from oil. Fry onion slices in hot oil till golden brown then add tomatoes, lemon grass, ginger, soy sauce, sugar and salt to taste. Stir-fry for 10 minutes before adding fish pieces, 1 cup water and coconut milk.

Simmer till gravy thickens, then add fried chillies and lemon juice. Cover pan and keep on very low heat. Remove pan from heat when gravy is almost completely absorbed. Serve fish with chillies on top, either with bread or rice.

Fish Malad

Baking : 20 mins.
Oven setting : 205 °C, 400 °F, Gas Regulo 8
Serves : 4

1 pound (450 g) threadfin (*ikan kurau*)
  or any boneless fish
salt to taste
2 teaspoons ground turmeric
3 tablespoons groundnuts
2 teaspoons coriander
2 tablespoons grated coconut
4 red chillies
2 stalks lemon grass
3 cloves garlic
3 slices ginger
2 teaspoons vinegar
¼ cup oil
3 onions, cut into rings
2 teaspoons sugar
3 green chillies, sliced
4 teaspoons chopped coriander leaves
1 tablespoon lemon juice

Cut fish into large pieces. Wash and rub with salt and ground turmeric. In a clean, dry pan, fry groundnuts over low heat till crisp. Stir continuously. Shell them and set aside. In the same manner, fry coriander and grated coconut for a few minutes. Grind coriander, coconut, groundnuts, red chillies, lemon grass, garlic and ginger with vinegar and 2 or 3 tablespoons water.

Heat oil in a pan over medium heat and lightly brown fish pieces. Remove to a dish. In the same oil, brown onion slices and remove to a dish. Add ground mixture, salt and sugar to the oil. Stir-fry for 5 minutes. Add 1 cup water and continue stir-frying till gravy is thick.

Place fish pieces in a casserole and completely cover with gravy, green chillies, chopped coriander leaves and fried onion. Bake in a moderately hot oven for 20 minutes. When done, sprinkle with lemon juice and serve with hot rice.

Fish Patori

Baking : 20 mins.
Oven setting : 205 °C, 400 °F, Regulo 8
Serves : 4

1 pound (450 g) fillet of threadfin (*ikan kurau*)
  or any fish
1 teaspoon salt
2 teaspoons ground turmeric
1 tablespoon mustard seed
2 red chillies, sliced
4 red chillies (for grinding)
1 tablespoon grated coconut
¼ cup oil
3 onions, sliced
1 tablespoon tomato puree
3 teaspoons chopped coriander leaves

Cut fish into 2-inch (5 cm) pieces, wash and rub with salt and ground turmeric. Set aside for 30 minutes. Grind mustard seed, 4 red chillies and grated coconut with ½ teaspoon salt. Keep the ground ingredients in an airtight container to preserve the flavour.

Heat oil in a pan over medium heat and fry onion slices till brown. Remove the pan from heat. Stir ground ingredients, tomato puree and salt into the onion and oil. Mix thoroughly. Coat fish pieces with this mixture. Place the whole lot in a casserole and sprinkle chilli slices on top. Bake in a moderate oven for 20 minutes.

When fish is done, garnish with chopped coriander leaves and serve with plain rice.

Moglai Fish Kabab

Oven setting : 205°C, 400°F, Gas Regulo 8
Serves   : 8

1 pound (450 g) fish fillet (any kind)
salt to taste
2 teaspoons ground turmeric
¾ cup melted ghee *or* oil
2 tablespoons ground turmeric
2 tablspoons *channa dhal*
2 onions, finely sliced
1 tablespoon ground chilli
2 teaspoons ginger jiuce
1 teaspoon *garam masala*
2 teaspoons roasted ground cummin
2 teaspoons plain white flour
2 teaspoons chopped coriander leaves
1 teaspoon sugar
2 eggs beaten
1 tablespoon yoghurt
1 tablespoon poppy seeds

Cut fish into big pieces. Wash and rub with salt and ground turmeric. Heat ½ cup oil in a pan over medium heat and fry fish pieces till brown. Remove from oil. When cool, mash with a fork. Soak *dhal* in water for 2 hours, then drain and grind finely. *Dhal* may be boiled with salt and dried.

Reheat oil in the pan and brown onion slices. Add ground or boiled *dhal,* ground chilli, ginger juice, *garam masala,* ground cummin, flour, chopped coriander leaves, sugar and salt to taste. Stir-fry this mixture for 10 minutes. Remove to a mixing bowl.

Mix fish, *dhal* mixture, beaten eggs, yoghurt and poppy seeds in the bowl. When well mixed, shape lumps of the mixture, the size of ping pong balls, into round patties. Place them on a greased baking sheet, sprinkle with ghee and bake in a moderately hot oven till golden brown. Serve hot with salad and a *chutney.*

Madras Fish Curry

Serves : 4

1 pound (450 g) threadfin (*ikan kurau*)
   or mackerel (*ikan tenggiri*)
salt to taste
2 teaspoons ground turmeric
6 dried chillies
2 teaspoons coriander
2 teaspoons sweet cummin
2 teaspoons cummin
4 cloves garlic
2 tablespoons oil
½ teaspoon mustard seed
3 onions, sliced
1½ cups coconut milk from ¼ pound (110 g)
   grated coconut
8 curry leaves
1 tablespoon tamarind juice
2 tomatoes, sliced

Cut fish into 2-inch (5 cm) pieces. Wash, season with salt and ground turmeric and set aside.

Heat a clean, dry pan over low heat and roast dried chillies, coriander, sweet cummin and cummin till chillies are dark brown. Stir continuously to ensure even roasting. Grind roasted ingredients with garlic.

Heat oil in a pan over medium heat and fry mustard seed and onions for 5 minutes or till onions are limp. Add 1 cup coconut milk, ground mixture, curry leaves and salt to taste. Stir-fry till mixture is almost dry, then add remaining coconut milk, fish and 1 cup water. Boil till fish is cooked. Finally, add tamarind juice and sliced tomatoes and remove from heat. Serve with plain rice.

Fish Kalia

Serves : 8

2 pounds (900 g) fillet of threadfin (*ikan kurau*)
salt to taste
2 teaspoons ground turmeric
½ cup oil
1 teaspoon cummin
2 sticks cinnamon
3 pods cardamom
2 onions, sliced
2-3 bay leaves
1 teaspoon sugar
1 onion, ground
1 tablespoon ground chilli
1 teaspoon ground cummin
1 teaspoon *garam masala*
1 teaspoon ginger juice
½ cup yoghurt
2 tomatoes, sliced

Cut fish into big pieces. Wash and rub with salt and ground turmeric. Set aside for 30 minutes. Heat oil in a pan over medium heat and brown fish pieces. Remove to a dish. The oil can be strained for the next stage.

In a clean saucepan, reheat strained oil on medium heat and fry cummin, cinnamon and cardamom for half a minute, then add onion slices and bay leaves and stir till onion slices are limp. Add sugar, ground ingredients, *garam masala*, ginger juice, yoghurt, ¼ cup cold water and salt to taste. Stir-fry till liquid dries up, and add fried fish and 2 cups cold water for gravy.

When fish is cooked and gravy thickened, add tomato slices and remove from heat. Serve with rice.

Spicy Fish Roast

Baking   : 30 mins.
Oven setting : 205°C, 400°F, Gas Regulo 8
Serves   : 6

1 whole grouper, about 1½ pounds (675 g)
5 or 6 *pandan* leaves
2 tablespoons cornflour
1 cup oil
1 stalk lemon grass, ground
4 cloves garlic, ground
2 onions, ground
1 tablespoon ground candlenuts
1 tablespoon ground chilli
2 teaspoons lemon juice

Clean and wash the fish. Rub all over with salt, wrap in *pandan* leaves and steam for 10 minutes over vigorously boiling water. Add a little water to cornflour to make a paste.

Remove leaves from the fish and rub all over with cornflour paste. Heat oil in a pan over medium heat and fry ground ingredients and salt to taste for 10 minutes. Place steamed fish in a casserole and pour fried ingredients over it. Bake in a moderately hot oven for 30 minutes till fish is brown and done. If necessary, put it under a grill for a further 5 minutes to make it crispy.

When fish is done, sprinkle with lemon juice and serve hot with a salad.

Note: The fish may be fried after steaming. Simply place it in the pan with fried ground ingredients and fry till brown. Stir ingredients carefully in the pan to prevent burning and to avoid breaking the fish.

Top — Parsi Chicken Roast
Bottom — Dhal Tikara
(Recipes: pp. 74, 17)

Top — Green Chilli Chicken
Bottom — Mutton Cutlet
(Recipes: pp. 73, 30)

Top — Rossogolla
Bottom — Mutton Vindaloo (left)
— Sweet Mango Chutney (right)
(Recipes: pp. 90, 60, 81)

Top left — Tandoori Fish
Top right — Sugar Cane Chicken
Bottom — Chapatis
(Recipes: pp. 35, 70, 13)

Fish Ferezi

Serves : 6

3 pounds (1350 g) threadfin (*ikan kurau*)
4 teaspoons ground turmeric
salt to taste
3 eggs, beaten
1 tablespoon cornflour
1 cup oil
½ cup yoghurt
2 teaspoons ground cummin
2 teaspoons ground ginger
2 tablespoons ground chilli
2 sticks cinnamon
4 pods cardamom
4 bay leaves
½ teaspoon cummin
1 teaspoon sugar
3 onions, ground
2 cloves garlic, chopped
2 onions, sliced
8 tomatoes, sliced
2 teaspoons chopped coriander leaves

Clean and skin the fish. Cut into large, thin pieces. Rub 2 teaspoons ground turmeric and salt into the pieces and let them soak in beaten eggs and cornflour for 30 minutes. Heat 1 cup of oil in a pan over medium heat and fry fish pieces till slightly brown. Remove the fish onto a dish and strain the oil. In a cup, mix 4 tablespoons water, ½ cup yoghurt, 2 teaspoons each of ground turmeric, ground cummin, ground ginger and 2 tablespoons ground chilli.

In a clean pan, heat 3 tablespoons oil over medium heat and fry cinnamon, cardamom, bay leaves and cummin for 1 minute. Then add sugar, ground onion and chopped garlic. Stir-fry till brown. Pour in the mixture of yoghurt and ground ingredients and onion slices. Stir till mixture is dry.

Add ½ cup hot water, stir for a minute, then add fried fish. Cook for about 10 minutes and when only a little gravy remains, add tomato slices. Remove from heat and serve garnished with chopped coriander leaves.

Fish Chatu

Serves : 4

1 pound (450 g) fish (any type)
salt to taste
2 teaspoons ground turmeric
1 tablespoon mustard seed
4 dried chillies
2 onions, sliced
2 green chillies, each cut into 2 or 3 sections
½ cup oil
2 teaspoons chopped coriander leaves

Clean fish, wash and rub with salt and ground turmeric. Set aside for 30 minutes. Grind mustard seed with dried chillies and ¼ teaspoon salt to a very smooth paste. Keep covered to preserve the flavour.

Bring 2 cups water in a pan to a boil and add fish, onions, ground paste and green chillies. Cover the pan and keep cooking on medium heat, opening occasionally to see if fish is cooked. In the meantime, bring ½ cup oil in a small container to a boil. When fish is cooked, add the hot oil to the ingredients in the pan and continue cooking on low heat till almost no liquid remains. Add chopped coriander leaves and remove from heat.

Fish Kabab

Serves : 8

1 pound (450 g) mackerel (*ikan tenggiri*)
   or herring (*ikan parang*)
oil for deep-fat frying
3 onions, chopped
2 green chillies, chopped
2 teaspoons ground ginger
1 teaspoon sugar
1 tablespoon ground chilli i
2 teaspoons roasted ground cummin
3 teaspoons chopped coriander leaves
1 tablespoon plain white flour
2 potatoes, boiled and mashed
1 teaspoon *garam masala*
breadcrumbs
2 eggs, beaten

Clean and wash fish. Steam till cooked. When cool, scrape flesh from bones and mash with a fork.

Heat 1 tablespoon oil in a pan over medium heat. Stir-fry onions, green chillies and ginger for 5 minutes, then add mashed fish, salt, sugar, ground chilli, ground cummin and chopped coriander leaves. Fry for 10 minutes, stirring all the while to mix well.

Remove fish mixture from heat and mix with flour, mashed potatoes and *garam masala*. Shape into round, flat patties of about 2-inch (5 cm) diameter. Coat with breadcrumbs, dip into beaten eggs and coat with breadcrumbs again. Deep-fry over medium heat till golden brown. Serve with a salad and tomato sauce.

Small Fish Jhall

Serves : 4

1 pound (450 g) sprats (*ikan tamban*)
salt to taste
1 teaspoon ground turmeric
½ cup oil
1 teaspoon black cummin
2 onions, sliced
1 tablespoon ground chilli
2 green chillies, sliced
2 teaspoons chopped coriander leaves

Clean fish, wash and season with salt and ground turmeric. Set aside for 30 minutes.

Heat oil in a frying pan (with a long handle) over medium heat and throw in black cummin. When cummin seeds are sputtering, add onion slices and stir-fry for 5 minutes. Pour in ¼ cup water and ground chilli. Fry till liquid dries up. Turn the heat down to low and toss in the fish. Do not stir with a spoon but shake the pan gently by the handle.

After 10 minutes, add ½ cup water, green chillies and salt to taste. Cook for a further 10 minutes. Throw in chopped coriander leaves and remove from heat. Serve with plain rice.

Dried Chilli Prawns

Serves : 6

2 pounds (900 g) medium-sized prawns
salt to taste
1 teaspoon sugar
2 teaspoons ground turmeric
¼ pound (110 g) dried chillies
2 onions, sliced
2 teaspoons ground ginger
1 stalk lemon grass, sliced
1 tablespoon tomato sauce
2 tablespoons first coconut milk
2 teaspoons lemon juice
2 teaspoons chopped spring onion

Shell, devein and wash prawns. Season with salt, sugar and ground turmeric. Set aside for 30 minutes.

Remove stems of dried chillies and fry in oil over medium heat till dark brown and puffy. Remove chillies from oil and stir-fry onion slices for 5 minutes. Add prawns and stir-fry till light brown, then add ginger, lemon grass and tomato sauce. Stir-fry for a few minutes, then pour in 2 cups water and coconut milk. Cook till gravy thickens and add lemon juice and fried chillies. Cover pan and simmer on very low heat. When about 1 cup gravy remains, season to taste and remove from heat.

Serve Dried Chilli Prawns with chillies on top and garnished with chopped spring onion. Serve with plain *pillau* and any *chutney*.

Prawn Curry

Serves : 8

2 pounds (900 g) large prawns
salt to taste
3 teaspoons ground turmeric
½ pound (225 g) potatoes
¼ cup oil
1 teaspoon cummin
2 sticks cinnamon
3 pods cardamom
3 onions, sliced
1 tablespoon ground chilli
2 teaspoons ground coriander
2 onions, ground
1 teaspoon ginger juice
½ cup yoghurt
1 teaspoon sugar
2 tomatoes, sliced

Shell, devein and wash prawns with salt water. Rub prawns with 2 teaspoons ground turmeric and 1 teaspoon salt. Set aside for 30 minutes. Skin and quarter large potatoes. Halve small ones. Rub with ½ teaspoon salt and 1 teaspoon ground turmeric. Fry in ¼ cup oil over medium heat till golden brown. Remove to a dish.

In the same hot oil, fry cummin, cinnamon and cardamom for 1 minute, then add sliced onions and stir-fry for a further 5 minutes. Add prawns, ground chilli, ground coriander, ground onions, ginger juice, yoghurt, sugar and salt to taste. Stir to mix well. Add 2 cups boiling water and potatoes and cook till potatoes are tender and the gravy is very thick. Now add sliced tomatoes and remove from heat. Serve with bread or rice.

Prawn Malai Curry

Serves : 8

2 pounds (900 g) large prawns
salt to taste
2 teaspoons ground turmeric
¼ cup oil
½ teaspoon cummin
2 sticks cinnamon
3 pods cardamom
8 onions, sliced
1 cup coconut milk from ½ pound (225 g) grated
  coconut
¼ cup yoghurt
1 onion, ground
1 tablespoon ground chilli
2 teaspoons ground cummin
2 teaspoons ginger juice
2 tomatoes, sliced
2 red chillies, halved

Shell, devein and wash prawns with salt water. Rub 1 teaspoon salt and ground turmeric into them and set aside for 30 minutes. Heat the oil in a *wok* and fry prawns till light brown. Remove to a dish.

In the same hot oil, fry cummin, cinnamon and cardamom for 1 minute, then add sliced onions and stir-fry for a further 5 minutes. Mix ½ cup coconut milk, yoghurt, ground onion, ground chilli, ground cummin and ginger juice in a bowl. Pour this mixture into the pan and stir-fry till mixture is almost dry. Add prawns, stir to mix well, then pour in remaining coconut milk. Cover the pan and cook over medium heat till gravy has thickened. Season to taste, add tomato slices and red chillies and serve with rice.

Prawn Korma

Serves : 4

1 pound (450 g) large prawns
salt to taste
2 teaspoons ground turmeric
2 tablespoons melted ghee *or* oil
1 teaspoon cummin
1 stick cinnamon
2 pods cardamom
3 teaspoons ground chilli
2 teaspoons ground cummin
1 teaspoon ground raisins
1 tablespoon ground almonds
1 teaspoon sugar
½ cup yoghurt
juice of 2 onions
2 teaspoons ginger juice
3 red chillies, halved

Shell, devein and wash prawns with salt water. Rub with ½ teaspoon salt and ground turmeric. Set aside for 30 minutes.

Heat ghee or oil and fry cummin, cinnamon and cardamom for 1 minute. Make sure the oil is not too hot. Then add ground chilli, ground cummin, ground raisins, ground almonds, sugar and a little salt. Stir-fry till almond turns light brown. Add prawns and yoghurt and stir-fry for a few minutes. Cover the pan and let contents simmer.

When liquid has dried up, add onion juice, ginger juice and ¼ cup water. Stir to mix, then cover pan again. As soon as prawns are cooked and only a little gravy remains, season to taste, add red chillies and remove from heat. Serve with bread or rice.

Dried Prawns Samburee

Serves : 6

1 pound (450 g) dried prawns
4 red chillies
2 inch (5 cm) piece ginger
¼ pound (110 g) roasted groundnuts
6 cloves garlic
1 stalk lemon grass
¼ pound (110 g) shallots
salt to taste
2 tablespoons oil
6 curry leaves
½ cup coconut milk from ½ pound (225 g)
   grated coconut
2 teaspoons lemon juice
1 tomato, sliced

Soak dried prawns in water for 30 minutes to soften. Drain well and roughly pound them. Grind chillies, ginger, groundnuts, garlic, lemon grass, half the shallots and ½ teaspoon salt together.

Slice the remaining shallots.

Heat oil in a pan over low heat and fry sliced shallots till brown. Add ground ingredients, curry leaves and prawns. Stir for 10 minutes, then add coconut milk. Simmer, stirring frequently, till gravy thickens. Add lemon juice and tomato slices, season to taste and remove from heat. Serve with rice.

Prawn and Cauliflower Kalia

Serves : 6

1 pound (450 g) large prawns
salt to taste
1 pound (450 g) cauliflower
½ pound (225 g) potatoes
4 teaspoons ground turmeric
¼ cup oil
½ teaspoon cummin
3 onions, sliced
¼ cup yoghurt
1 tablespoon ground chilli
1 tablespoon ground cummin
1 teaspoon sugar
1 teaspoon *garam masala*
¼ cup cooked green peas

Shell, devein and wash prawns in salt water. Rub with ½ teaspoon salt and 1 teaspoon ground turmeric. Set aside for 30 minutes. Cut cauliflower into big pieces. Peel and halve big potatoes, leaving small ones whole. Season cauliflower and potatoes with 1 teaspoon salt and 2 teaspoons ground turmeric.

Heat oil in a pan over medium heat and fry cauliflower and potatoes till the potatoes are brown. Remove to a dish. Fry prawns in the same oil for 5 minutes and remove these to the same dish.

In the same oil, stir-fry cummin and sliced onions for 10 minutes. Add ½ cup water, yoghurt, ground chilli, ground cummin, sugar and salt to taste. Stir till liquid dries up, then add prawns, cauliflower, potatoes and 1 cup water for gravy. Cover the pan and allow to simmer. When potatoes are tender, add *garam masala* and cooked peas. Remove from heat when only a little gravy remains. Serve with *loochi* or bread.

Stuffed Crab

Baking : *30 mins.*
Oven setting : *150°C, 300°F, Gas Regulo 4*
Serves : *6*

2 pounds (900 g) large crabs
salt to taste
¼ cup ghee *or* oil
3 onions, finely chopped
4 cloves garlic, finely chopped
2 teaspoons ground ginger
1 tablespoon ground chilli
2 teaspoons roasted ground cummin
1 teaspoon sugar
1 teaspoon *garam masala*
3 teaspoons chopped coriander leaves
2 eggs, beaten
breadcrumbs

Remove all unwanted parts of crabs and wash thoroughly. Boil the crabs with 1 teaspoon salt in sufficient water to cover. When cooked, allow to cool. Extract the flesh and chop finely. Wash crab shells and dry them with a tea towel.

Heat ghee or oil in a pan over medium heat and fry onions, garlic and ginger till light brown. Add crabmeat, ground chilli, ground cummin, sugar, salt to taste and ¼ cup water. Stir till dry. Add *garam masala* and coriander, mix thoroughly and remove from heat.

Fill crab shells with crabmeat mixture. Brush the crabmeat generously with beaten egg, cover with breadcrumbs and bake in a moderate oven till brown. Serve with chilli sauce and a salad.

Prawn Malad

Baking : *30 mins.*
Oven setting : *205°C, 400°F, Gas Regulo 8*
Serves : *6*

1 pound (450 g) medium-sized prawns
salt to taste
1 tablespoon mustard seed
6 red chillies, 2 of them coarsely sliced
2 tablespoons grated coconut
¼ cup oil
1 teaspoon sugar
2 teaspoons ground turmeric
1 tablespoon tomato puree
3 onions, sliced
1 piece banana leaf large enough to cover the
    bottom of a casserole (optional)
2 teaspoons chopped coriander leaves

Shell, devein and wash prawns with salt water to remove sliminess. Grind mustard seed, 4 chillies, grated coconut and ¼ teaspoon salt to a paste. Heat the oil till it is almost boiling.

Mix prawns, ground mixture, sugar, ground turmeric, tomato puree, onion slices and salt to taste. Spread the banana leaf at the bottom of a casserole and pour prawn mixture on top of it. Bake for about 30 minutes in a moderately hot oven. When cooked, sprinkle with chopped coriander leaves and serve with hot rice.

Meat

Seekh Kabab

Baking   : 50 mins.
Oven setting : 150°C, 300°F, Gas Regulo 4
Serves   : 6

2 pounds (900 g) minced mutton
1 tablespoon grated coconut
2 onions
2 inch (5 cm) piece ginger
4 cloves garlic
1 tablespoon *channa dhal* flour
2 teaspoons ground cummin
1 teaspoon *garam masala*
2 tablespoons plain white flour
1 tablespoon ground chilli
1 egg, beaten
3 teaspoons chopped coriander leaves
1 teaspoon sugar
salt to taste
a little melted ghee
1 teaspoon lemon juice
1 tablespoon yoghurt
3 onions, cut into rings
6 metal skewers

Grind or pound minced mutton with grated coconut, onions, ginger and garlic. Then mix with *dhal* flour, ground cummin, *garam masala,* white flour, ground chilli, beaten egg, chopped coriander leaves, sugar, salt and lemon juice. Knead well for about 10 minutes.

Rub hot skewers with an absorbent cloth which has been dipped into melted ghee.

Then wrap one-sixth of the meat mixture around each skewer in the shape of a sausage. Brush generously with yoghurt and roast in a moderate oven for 50 minutes till golden brown. Serve with onion rings and *chutney.*

Seekh Kabab in Pieces

Serves : 6

2 pounds (900 g) lean meat, any kind
1 ounce (30 g) poppy seed
5 cloves garlic
2 onions
6 dried chillies
1 teaspoon coriander
2 inch (5 cm) piece ginger
salt to taste
2 teaspoons ground cummin
1 teaspoon sugar
¼ cup yoghurt
1 teaspoon *garam masala*
melted ghee *or* butter
2 tomatoes, cut into rings
2 onions, cut into rings
1 lemon, cut into rings
some metal skewers

Grind poppy seed, garlic, onions, dried chillies, coriander and ginger with salt. Add ground cummin, sugar, yoghurt and *garam masala.* Mix well to get a paste. Marinate meat in this for 4-5 hours. Thread the strips onto metal skewers and grill till brown. Baste with melted ghee or butter once in a while, if necessary.

Wash meat and cut into thin strips 2 inches (5 cm) wide and 3 inches (7 ½ cm) long. Leave on a clean tea towel to dry.

Serve with *chapati* or bread, tomato, onion and lemon rings.

Grilled Mutton or Lamb Kabab

Oven setting : 150°C, 300°F, Gas Regulo 4
Serves   : 6

2 pounds (900 g) mutton *or* lamb
½ cup yoghurt
1 teaspoon sugar
4 cloves garlic, ground
2 teaspoons ground ginger
1 onion, ground
3 tablespoons chilli sauce
salt to taste
some jacket onions, peeled
juice of 1 lemon
2 ounces (60 g) melted butter
6 metal skewers

sugar, ground ingredients, chilli sauce and salt for 4 hours.

Arrange meat cubes and jacket onions alternately on greased skewers, ending with a cube of meat. Brush generously with melted butter and bake in a moderately hot oven or grill till brown. When done, sprinkle with lemon juice and serve hot with a salad.

Cut meat into 1-inch (2 ½ cm) cubes. Wash and dry. Marinate in yoghurt,

Kabab with Gravy

Serves : 6

2 pounds (900 g) mutton
2 tablespoons yoghurt
2 teaspoons ground ginger
2 teaspoons ground garlic
1 tablespoon ground onion
1 tablespoon ground chilli
2 teaspoons ground poppy seed
2 teaspoons ground coriander
2 teaspoons black sauce
2 teaspoons sugar
salt to taste
1 ounce (30 g) cooking fat
3 onions, cut into rings
some metal skewers

Cut mutton into thin slices. Boil in just a little water till half-cooked and almost dry. Remove from heat and drain away all liquid.

Marinate boiled mutton in a mixture of all the ingredients (except cooking fat and onion rings) for 4-5 hours. Thread onto metal skewers and grill under a pre-heated grill, basting continuously with melted fat till mutton is cooked. Collect gravy which forms in a pan. Serve grilled kababs with onion rings and gravy.

Kashmiri Kabab

Serves : 8

2 pounds (900 g) lean mutton
salt to taste
1 teaspoon sugar
juice of 4 cloves garlic
juice of 2 onions
2 teaspoons ginger juice
1 tablespoon ground chilli
2 teaspoons ground coriander
2 teaspoons vinegar
¼ cup yoghurt
1 teaspoon *garam masala*
2 tablespoons rice flour
4 tablespoons *dhal* flour
2 beaten eggs
2 teaspoons ground mustard seed
4-5 onions, cut into rings ¼ inch (½ cm) thick
some toothpicks, split in half
ghee *or* oil for deep-fat frying

Cut mutton into thin strips about 2 inches (5 cm) by 3 inches (7 ½ cm). Boil

with salt, sugar, garlic juice, onion juice, ginger juice, ground chilli, ground coriander, vinegar and yoghurt. Cover and simmer till mutton is tender and no gravy remains. Stir in *garam masala* and remove from heat.

In a bowl, mix rice flour and *dhal* flour with beaten eggs, ground mustard seed and salt. If batter is too thick, add a little water. Beat well. Take 2 onion rings and put a meat slice, folded to fit, between them. Join with two toothpick halves, dip in batter and deep-fry till golden brown. Serve with salad.

Moglai Meat Kabab

Baking   : *50 mins.*
Oven setting : *150°C, 300°F, Gas Regulo 4*
Serves   : *6*

1 pound (450 g) minced mutton
salt to taste
2 teaspoons vinegar
2 tablespoons *channa dhal*
3 tablespoons melted ghee
3 onions, finely chopped
1 teaspoon sugar
1 teaspoon ground chilli
2 teaspoons ginger juice
2 teaspoons roasted ground cummin
2 teaspoons chopped coriander leaves
2 teaspoons plain white flour
1 teaspoon *garam masala*
2 eggs, beaten
2 onions, cut into rings

Boil minced mutton with salt and vinegar in a little water. Cook until dry. Soak *dhal* in cold water for 2 hours to soften, then drain off water and grind to a paste. *Dhal* can be boiled also.

Heat 2 tablespoons melted ghee in a pan over medium heat and fry chopped onion till limp, then remove from oil. In the same oil, fry ground *dhal,* salt, sugar, ground chilli, ginger juice, ground cummin, chopped coriander leaves, poppy seed, white flour and *garam masala.* Stir-fry for 10 or 20 minutes, then remove from heat.

Mix boiled mutton with *dhal* mixture, fried onion and beaten eggs. Knead well and divide into small balls of about 1½ inch (4 cm) diameter. Grease a baking sheet and place all kababs on the sheet. Sprinkle or brush a little melted ghee on them and bake in a moderately hot oven till golden brown. Serve with onion rings and sauce.

Note: Kababs may be fried if desired.

Shammi Kabab

Serves : 12

2 pounds (900 g) minced mutton
½ pound (225 g) *channa dhal*
5 cloves garlic, chopped
4 inch (5 cm) piece ginger, chopped
6 dried chillies
1 tablespoon poppy seed
2 teaspoons cummin
2 teaspoons coriander
2 sticks cinnamon
8 pods cardamom
1 teaspoon sugar
salt to taste
7 onions, finely sliced
2 eggs, beaten
1 teaspoon *garam masala*
3 teaspoons chopped coriander leaves
1 tablespoon plain white flour
2 teaspoons roasted ground cummin
2 teaspoons lemon juice
4 green chillies, chopped
ghee *or* oil for deep-fat frying

Boil mutton with *dhal,* garlic, ginger, dried chillies, poppy seed, cummin, coriander, cinnamon, cardamom, sugar and salt. When *dhal* is cooked and liquid dried up, remove from heat.

Heat ¼ cup ghee over medium heat and fry sliced onions till slightly brown. Remove half the quantity of onions to a dish and continue frying remaining onions till dark brown and crispy.

Grind or pound boiled meat mixture with crispy fried onions and mix in beaten eggs, *garam masala,* chopped coriander leaves, white flour and ground cummin. Make small balls of about 1 ½ inch (4 cm) diameter. Shape into a cup and place in the centre a little fried onion, lemon juice, a little salt and chopped green chilli. Draw in the rim of the cup and pat into flat, round shapes. Deep-fry a few at a time over low heat till dark brown. Drain well and serve with salad and *chutney.*

Madras Mutton Curry

Serves : 8

2 pounds (900 g) mutton
8 dried chillies
2 teaspoons cummin
3 teaspoons sweet cummin
3 teaspoons coriander
8 curry leaves
2 inch (5 cm) piece ginger
salt to taste
½ cup first coconut milk and 1 cup second coco-
    nut milk from 1 pound (450 g) grated coconut
3 onions, sliced
5 cloves garlic, chopped
2 teaspoons ground turmeric
1 tablespoon tamarind juice
2 sticks cinnamon
1 tablespoon butter *or* oil
4 pods cardamom

Cut mutton into small pieces. Wash and put aside. Remove stems of dried chillies. Heat a clean, dry pan over very low heat and roast dried chillies with cummin, 2 teaspoons sweet cummin, coriander and curry leaves till chillies are puffy and dark brown. Stir continuously in a 'down the side and up the centre' movement so that all ingredients are heated evenly. Grind roasted ingredients with ginger.

Boil mutton with salt, second coconut milk, 1 tablespoon onion slices, half the chopped garlic, half the ground turmeric, and a little water in a covered pan. When mutton is cooked, add ground ingredients, tamarind juice and first coconut milk. Boil for 5 minutes and remove from heat.

In a clean pan, heat butter or oil and fry remaining sweet cummin, cinnamon and cardamom for 1 minute, then add remaining garlic and onions and fry till brown. Pour in mutton curry and allow to simmer for a further 5 minutes. Serve hot with rice.

Minced Mutton Curry

Serves : 4

¼ cup oil
2 potatoes, cubed
1 teaspoon cummin
1 stick cinnamon
3 pods cardamom
3 cloves garlic, thinly sliced
1 onion, sliced
1 pound (450 g) minced mutton
salt to taste
1 teaspoon sugar
2 teaspoons ground chilli
1 teaspoon ground coriander
2 teaspoons ground turmeric
1 teaspoon ground cummin
2 tomatoes, sliced
¼ cup cooked green peas
2 teaspoons chopped coriander leaves

Heat oil in a pan over medium heat and fry potato cubes till golden brown. Remove to a bowl. In the same oil, fry cummin, cinnamon and cardamom for 1 minute, then add garlic and onion and stir-fry till light brown.

Add mutton, salt, sugar and ground ingredients. Stir-fry till mixture is dry, then add 4 cups water, potatoes and tomatoes. Cover the pan and simmer till mutton is cooked. Add green peas and chopped coriander leaves. Stir well and remove from heat. Serve with *chapati* or bread.

Dry Mutton Curry

Serves : 8

2 pounds (900 g) mutton chop
¼ cup yoghurt *or* first coconut milk (2 teaspoons lemon juice to be added to coconut milk, if used)
2 teaspoons ground ginger
1 teaspoon ground garlic
3 onions, finely sliced
1 teaspoon black peppercorns, crushed
1 teaspoon sugar
salt to taste
1 tablespoon ghee *or* oil
1 teaspoon sweet cummin
2 sticks cinnamon
4 pods cardamom
10 shallots, peeled and left whole
6 green chillies, halved
3 tomatoes, sliced

Cut mutton into small pieces, wash and drain dry. Marinate in yoghurt or coconut milk, ground ginger, ground garlic, half the quantity of onion slices, crushed black pepper, sugar and salt. Marinate meat for 4 hours.

Heat ghee or oil in a pan over medium heat and fry sweet cummin, cinnamon and cardamom for 1 minute. Add remaining onion slices and stir till light brown. Add mutton and marinade, stir well, cover the pan and simmer. Stir occasionally to prevent burning. When liquid has dried up, add 6 cups water and continue cooking on low heat till mutton is cooked and tender. (If a pressure cooker is used, add 1 cup water.)

Add shallots and green chillies. Simmer for another 5 minutes, then add tomato slices and remove from heat. Serve with bread or rice.

Mutton Shahi Korma

Serves : 8

2 pounds (900 g) mutton chops
2 teaspoons vinegar
1 teaspoon ginger juice
2 teaspoons ground coriander
2 teaspoons ground cummin
1 tablespoon ground chilli
3 onions, sliced
1 teaspoon sugar
salt to taste
2 sticks cinnamon
4 pods cardamom
5 cloves garlic, chopped
2 teaspoons ground raisins
10 almonds, ground
½ cup yoghurt
12 shallots
1 tablespoon ghee *or* oil

Clean, wash and dry mutton chops. Cut into large 2-inch (1 cm) thick pieces. Marinate in vinegar, ginger juice, ground coriander, ground cummin, ground chilli, 1 tablespoon onion slices, sugar and salt for 4 hours.

Heat ghee or oil in a pan over medium heat and fry cinnamon and cardamom for 1 minute. Then add garlic, remaining onion slices, ground raisins, and ground almonds and stir till light brown. Add mutton and stir-fry till liquid dries up. Add ¼ cup yoghurt and 2 cups water. (If a pressure cooker is used, add only 1 cup water.) Stir well. Cover the pan and simmer, stirring occasionally. When very little gravy remains, add shallots and cook for another 5 minutes. Season to taste. Serve hot korma with *chapati,* plain rice or bread.

Mutton Vindaloo

Serves : 8

2 pounds (900 g) mutton
salt to taste
2 teaspoons honey
½ cup yoghurt
2 teaspoons vinegar
a few drops of yellow food colouring
juice of 2 onions
4 cloves garlic, ground
2 teaspoons ground ginger
1 tablespoon ghee *or* oil
½ teaspoon sweet cummin
2 sticks cinnamon
4 pods cardamom
1 onion, sliced
1 tablespoon grated coconut, finely ground
3 teaspoons ground chilli
1 tablespoon roasted ground coriander
½ pound (225 g) shallots, peeled and left whole
1 tablespoon tomato puree
½ pound (225 g) potatoes (optional)

Cut mutton into big pieces. Wash, dry and prick all over with a fork. Marinate in a mixture of salt, honey, yoghurt, vinegar, yellow food colouring and onion juice for 4 hours. Mix ground garlic and ginger with ½ cup water.

Heat ghee or oil in a pan over medium heat and fry sweet cummin, cinnamon and cardamom for 1 minute. Add sliced onion and fry till light brown. Add ground coconut, ground chilli and ground coriander. Stir-fry for half a minute, then add ½ cup water. Stir till liquid has almost dried up. Add mutton and marinade. Cover the pan and continue cooking on medium heat.

When mutton is three-quarters cooked, add ginger and garlic mixture. Stir for 5 minutes to mix well. If necessary, add ½ cup water. Finally add shallots and tomato puree. Cook for another 20 minutes on very low heat. Serve with *pillau* or *chapati.*

Note: Potatoes may be added to Vindaloo if desired. Boil in salt water and when three-quarters cooked, remove from heat and allow to cool. Peel off skin and fry in oil till brown, then add to Vindaloo with ginger and garlic. Also, pork or beef may be used instead of mutton.

Mutton Kalia

Serves : 8

2 pounds (900 g) mutton
2 teaspoons vinegar
3 teaspoons ginger juice
½ cup yoghurt
3 teaspoons ground chilli
2 teaspoons ground sweet cummin
2 teaspoons ground turmeric
salt to taste
½ pound (225 g) potatoes
3 teaspoons ghee *or* oil
½ teaspoon sweet cummin
2 sticks cinnamon
4 pods cardamom
4 cloves garlic, chopped
1 teaspoon sugar
4 onions, sliced
3 bay leaves
3 teaspoons chopped coriander leaves
3 teaspoons tomato puree
2 tomatoes, sliced

Wash and cut mutton into 2-inch (5 cm) pieces. Marinate in a mixture of vinegar, ginger juice, yoghurt, ground chilli, ground cummin, 1½ teaspoons ground turmeric and salt. Keep covered for 2 hours. Peel potatoes, cut into bite-sized pieces and rub with salt and ½ teaspoon ground turmeric.

Heat oil in a pan over medium heat and fry potatoes till golden brown. Remove to a dish. In the same oil, fry sweet cummin, cinnamon, cardamom, garlic and sugar for 1 minute. Add sliced onions and bay leaves and stir-fry for 10 minutes. Then add mutton, stir well and cover the pan. Simmer over low heat, stirring occasionally.

When liquid has dried up, stir in chopped coriander leaves and tomato puree. Add 2 cups water and continue simmering till mutton is tender. Add potatoes, cook for another 10 minutes, then add sliced tomatoes. Remove the pan from heat while there is still a little gravy left. Serve with rice or *chapati*.

Meat Kofta Curry

Serves : 6

3 green chillies
1 inch (2½ cm) piece ginger
4 cloves garlic
1 onion
1 pound (450 g) finely minced mutton
6 teaspoons *garam masala*
2 teaspoons plain white flour
1 teaspoon sugar
salt to taste
oil for deep-fat frying
2 potatoes, cubed
1 teaspoon cummin
1 stick cinnamon
3 pods cardamom
2 onions, sliced
2 teaspoons ground turmeric
3 teaspoons ground chilli
3 teaspoons ground cummin
¼ cup yoghurt
2 tomatoes, sliced

Grind green chillies, ginger, garlic and onion. Mix with mutton. Add *garam masala,* flour, 1 teaspoon sugar and salt.

Knead well and shape into small balls of 1 inch (2½ cm) diameter. Heat oil for deep-fat frying over medium heat and fry kofta balls in hot oil till dark brown. Drain well.

In the same oil, fry potatoes till light brown. Remove to a bowl. Pour out all but 2 tablespoons oil. Fry cummin, cinnamon and cardamom for one minute, then add sliced onions and stir-fry till light brown. Add ground turmeric, ground chilli, ground cummin, yoghurt, 1 teaspoon sugar and salt. Stir till liquid dries up, then add 2 cups water, potatoes, meatballs and boil till meatballs are cooked and potatoes tender. Toss in tomato slices and remove from heat when only about ½ cup thick gravy remains. Serve with bread or rice.

Lamb with Almonds

Serves : 6

2 tablespoons butter *or* ghee
4 cm (1½ in) stick cinnamon
4 pods cardamom
2 large onions, chopped
4 cloves garlic, chopped
1 inch (2½ cm) piece ginger, chopped
3 dried chillies
900 g (2 lb) lamb, cut into bite-sized cubes
1 teaspoon *garam masala*
½ cup yoghurt
1 drop yellow colouring
2 teaspoons ground chilli
¼ cup ground almond
2 cups water
1 teaspoon sugar
salt to taste
½ cup thick coconut milk
2 tomatoes, sliced into rings
1 onion, sliced into thin rings

Melt butter or ghee in a saucepan over low heat. Stir-fry cinnamon, cardamom and cloves for 1 minute, then add onions, garlic, ginger, dried chillies and stir-fry till brown.

Mix lamb with *garam masala* and add to contents of saucepan. Stir-fry till meat turns light brown before adding yoghurt, yellow colouring, ground chilli, ground almond, 2 tablespoons water, sugar and salt to taste.

When dry, add coconut milk and remaining water. Cook covered till meat is tender and gravy is thick. Remove from heat and garnish with tomato and onion rings.

Serve with plain rice or bread.

Top left — Mutton Kachuri
Top right — Loochi
Bottom — Eggplant Pur Bhaji
(Recipes: pp. 107, 18, 111)

Left — Mattar Panir
Right — Egg Doh Piazi
(Recipes: pp. 25, 34)

Dry Chilli Fish (Recipe: p. 39)

Top left — Egg Devil
Top right: Bhindi Curry
Bottom: Sago Pillau
(Recipes: pp. 33, 24, 116)

Sweet Sour Lamb

Serves : 8

2 pounds (900 g) lamb chop
salt to taste
2 teaspoons vinegar
6 cloves garlic, ground
1 tablespoon ground onion
2 teaspoons ground ginger
2 tablespoons cornflour
3 teaspoons ground chilli
2 eggs, beaten
oil
1 cup fresh pineapple cubes (use tinned
    pineapple if fresh pineapple is not available)
1 large carrot, cut into thin rings
2 onions, sliced
3 red chillies, chopped
2 tablespoons brown sugar
2 tablespoons malt vinegar
2 teaspoons soy sauce
1 tablespoon sherry
1 teaspoon ground pepper
1 tablespoon tomato puree
1 small cucumber, sliced
1 tablespoon sliced celery

Cut lamb into thin slices and marinate in salt, vinegar, ground garlic, ground onion, ground ginger and 1 cup water for 30 minutes. Put lamb with marinade in a saucepan and simmer over low heat till lamb is half-cooked and dry. A pressure cooker may be used, if desired. Remove from heat.

Heat 2 tablespoons oil in a clean pan over medium heat and fry pineapple cubes and carrot rings for 10 minutes. Remove to a dish. In the same hot oil, fry onion slices and chillies for 5 minutes. Mix ½ tablespoon cornflour with ½ cup water, brown sugar, salt, malt vinegar, soy sauce and sherry. Pour this mixture into the pan together with cooked pineapple and carrot. Boil for 5 minutes, stirring till gravy thickens. Add fresh lamb pieces, pepper and tomato puree and remove from heat. Garnish with cucumber and celery and serve with plain rice.

Mix 1 tablespoon cornflour, ground chilli, beaten eggs, 1 tablespoon water and salt together. Beat wtih a fork to mix well. Heat 1 cup oil in a pan over medium heat. Dip lamb pieces in batter and fry in hot oil till brown.

Spicy Mutton Soup

Serves : 4

1 pound (450 g) mutton chop
4 cloves garlic, chopped
3 teaspoons chopped ginger
1 stick cinnamon
4 pods cardamom
2 teaspoons coriander
4 teaspoons red lentils (*masoor dhal*)
2 teaspoons sweet cummin
1 teaspoon crushed black pepper
salt to taste
2 tomatoes, quartered
2 teaspoons chopped spring onion
2 teaspoons chopped coriander leaves
4 teaspoons oil
1 onion, chopped

Wash and cut mutton into large pieces. Tie all other ingredients except tomatoes, spring onion, coriander leaves and onion in a piece of muslin. Boil 8 cups water in a saucepan. Put in mutton, spice bag and salt. When water comes to a boil once more, turn down heat and simmer till mutton is tender and liquid is reduced to a third of the original amount. Add tomatoes, chopped spring onion, chopped coriander leaves and continue simmering for 5 minutes, on very low heat.

Heat oil in a clean pan and fry chopped onions till golden brown. Add to boiling soup just before serving.

Poultry

Tandoori Chicken

Oven setting : 500°F
Serves   : 8

1 chicken, about 3 pounds (1350 g)
2 teaspoons vinegar
1½ cups yoghurt
4 teaspoons butter *or* ghee
1 tablespoon ground onion
4 cloves garlic, ground
½ tablespoon ginger juice
3 teaspoons tomato puree
2 teaspoons ground coriander
2 teaspoons ground chilli
2 teaspoons ground mustard
1 teaspoon sugar
salt to taste
1 onion, cut into rings

Clean, wash and dry chicken. Skin the whole chicken and cut off the neck and wings. Make 3 or 4 diagonal cuts into the breast and legs, about halfway down to the bone. Use a fork to prick all over, as far into the chicken as possible. Rub in vinegar and salt and leave for 1 hour.

Prepare the marinade. Mix all these ingredients in a bowl large enough to hold the chicken: yoghurt, butter or ghee, onion, garlic, ginger juice, tomato puree, coriander, chilli, mustard, sugar and salt to taste. Marinate the chicken in this mixture for 4 hours. Turn the chicken a few times during this period to ensure even marinating.

Grease a baking tray and bake chicken for about 1 hour in a moderately hot oven. Turn the chicken occasionally and baste with the marinade. Spread onion rings all over the chicken about halfway through the baking. When chicken is done, remove from the oven, sprinkle lemon juice all over and serve with salad and naan.

Chicken in Sugar Cane

Oven setting : 205°C, 400°F, Gas Regulo 8
Serves   : 8

1 chicken, about 3 pounds (1350 g)
½ cup yoghurt
juice from 2 onions
6 cloves garlic, ground
1 tablespoon ground ginger
4 red chillies, ground
2 tablespoons cornflour
3 teaspoons red wine
a few drops of orange food colouring
2 teaspoons salt
4 segments sugar cane (to make 3 cups of smaller
    pieces)
1 tablespoon butter

Clean and wash whole chicken. Dry it. In a bowl, mix yoghurt, onion juice, ground garlic, ground ginger, ground chillies, cornflour, red wine, orange food colouring and salt. Rub the mixture all over chicken, inside and out, and set aside for 2 hours.

Use a pointed knife to pry out the tough sugar cane casing. Discard the tough joints and cut into 2 inch (5 cm) lengths. Quarter each piece lengthwise to make 3 cups of small sugar cane pieces. Stuff 1 cup sugar cane into the cavity of the chicken and sew up the opening.

Place chicken on a baking tray. Spread out remaining sugar cane around it on the tray. Brush chicken generously with butter and bake in a moderately hot oven till golden brown. Remove from oven, cut chicken into pieces and arrange with sugar cane pieces on a flat dish.

Milk Chicken

Serves : 8

1 chicken, about 3 pounds (1350 g)
2 cups coconut milk from 1 pound (450 g)
    grated coconut
1 stalk lemon grass, crushed
2 teaspoons chopped ginger
4 cloves garlic, sliced
1 teaspoon crushed black pepper
salt to taste
1 tablespoon roasted cashew-nuts
5 red chillies, halved
1 tablespoon oil
2 onions, sliced
2 teaspoons chopped parsley
4 tomatoes, sliced
2 teaspoons lemon juice

Cut chicken into large pieces, wash and drain well. Bring 2 cups water to a boil in a saucepan. Add chicken, coconut milk, lemon grass, ginger, garlic, pepper and salt. When this comes to a boil, cover the pan and lower heat.

When chicken is three-quarters cooked, add cashew-nuts and chillies. Cook for a few more minutes. In the meantime, heat oil in a pan· over medium heat and fry sliced onions till light brown. Add browned onion slices, chopped parsley and tomato slices to chicken and continue simmering for a further 5 minutes. Add lemon juice. Remove from heat and serve with rice or bread.

Bengal Chicken Curry

Serves : 8

1 chicken, about 2 pounds (900 g)
2 teaspoons ground turmeric
½ cup yoghurt
1 teaspoon sugar
salt to taste
½ pound (225 g) potatoes
¼ cup melted ghee *or* oil
½ teaspoon cummin
2 sticks cinnamon
4 pods cardamom
4 cloves garlic, chopped
1 onion, sliced
juice of 1 onion
2 teaspoons ginger juice
3 teaspoons ground chilli
2 teaspoons ground cummin
2-3 bay leaves
4 tomatoes, quartered

Cut chicken into large pieces. Wash, drain and marinate in 1 teaspoon ground turmeric, yoghurt, sugar and salt. Peel and cut potatoes into big pieces and rub with salt and remaining ground turmeric.

Heat ghee or oil in a pan over medium heat and fry potatoes till slightly browned. Remove from oil. In the same hot oil, fry cummin, cinnamon and cardamom for 1 minute, then add chopped garlic and sliced onion and stir-fry till light brown. Add chicken, onion juice, ginger juice, ground chilli, ground cummin and bay leaves. Stir well.

Cover the pan and simmer till liquid has dried up. Add 3 cups water, stir to mix ingredients and cover the pan again. When chicken is cooked, add potatoes and cook for a further 20 minutes. Finally, add tomatoes and remove pan from heat. Gravy should be thick. Serve with plain rice or bread.

Chicken Mailu

Serves : 6

1 chicken, about 2 pounds (900 g)
¼ cup yoghurt
1 teaspoon sugar
salt to taste
4 tablespoons melted butter
½ teaspoon cummin
2 sticks cinnamon
3 pods cardamom
4 cloves garlic, chopped
4 red chillies, halved
1 teaspoon ground turmeric
2 teaspoons ginger juice
juice of 3 onions
¼ cup thin milk, evaporated
2 tomatoes, sliced

Cut chicken into 8 pieces. Wash and rub

pieces with yoghurt, sugar and salt. Set aside for 2 hours.

Heat butter in a pan over medium heat and lightly fry cummin, cinnamon, cardamom and chopped garlic. Then add chicken, chillies, ground turmeric, ginger juice and onion juice. Fry till liquid has dried up. Stir in milk and ½ cup water for gravy. Lower heat and cover the pan. Simmer, stirring occasionally, till chicken is tender, then add tomatoes. Remove from heat when a little gravy remains. Serve with rice or bread.

71

Chicken Korma

Serves : 8

1 chicken, about 3 pounds (1350 g)
1 tablespoon ginger juice
½ cup yoghurt
1 tablespoon ground chilli
2 teaspoons ground coriander
4 onions, sliced
1 teaspoon sugar
salt to taste
2 tablespoons melted ghee *or* oil
2 sticks cinnamon
4 pods cardamom
5 cloves garlic, chopped
15 almonds, ground
2 teaspoons raisins, ground
¼ cup milk, evaporated
12 shallots, peeled and left whole

Clean, wash and cut chicken into large pieces. Leave on a clean tea towel for 20 minutes to dry. Marinate the pieces in a mixture of ginger juice, yoghurt, ground chilli, ground coriander, 1 tablespoon onion slices, sugar and salt. Leave chicken in the marinade for 4 hours.

Heat ghee or oil in a pan over medium heat and fry cinnamon, cardamom, remaining sliced onions and chopped garlic till brown. Add ground almonds and raisins and stir-fry with a little water for a few minutes. Put in chicken and stir well. Cover the pan and cook on medium heat, stirring occasionally to prevent burning.

When chicken is dry, add milk and 2 cups water. Cover the pan and continue simmering till chicken is tender. Add shallots and continue cooking till all liquid is absorbed and very thick dry gravy remains. Serve korma hot with *chapati* or plain rice.

Chilli Chicken

Serves : 6

1 chicken, about 2 pounds (900 g)
½ cup yoghurt
1 teaspoon sugar
salt to taste
1 tablespoon poppy seeds
1 tablespoon grated coconut
5 red chillies
6 cloves garlic
1 inch (2½ cm) piece ginger
3 teaspoons chopped coriander leaves
4 onions, sliced
2 tablespoons ghee *or* oil
½ teaspoon sweet cummin
2 teaspoons lemon juice
2 tomatoes, sliced

Cut chicken into small pieces and rub in yoghurt, sugar and salt. Grind the following together: poppy seeds, grated coconut, red chillies, garlic, ginger, coriander leaves and 1 tablespoon onion slices.

Heat ghee or oil in a pan over medium heat and fry sweet cummin and remaining sliced onions till brown. Add ground ingredients and stir-fry for 5 minutes. Add ½ cup water and continue stirring for a few more minutes, then add chicken and mix well. Lower heat and cover the pan. Simmer, stirring occasionally, till chicken is tender and liquid has dried up. Add lemon juice and tomatoes and remove from heat. Serve with a salad.

Green Chilli Chicken

Serves : 8

1 chicken, about 3 pounds (1350 g)
½ cup yoghurt
2 onions, ground
2 teaspoons ground ginger
6 cloves ground garlic
3 teaspoons ground cummin
1 teaspoon crushed black pepper
1 teaspoon sugar
salt to taste
2 pounds (900 g) green chillies
¼ cup melted butter *or* oil
2 sticks cinnamon
4 pods cardamom
2 onions, sliced
1 tablespoon lemon juice

Cut chicken into large pieces and wash well. Marinate chicken in a mixture of yoghurt, ground ingredients, crushed black pepper, sugar and salt. Keep

covered for 4 hours. In the meantime, remove stems of green chillies and wash them.

Heat butter or oil in a pan over medium heat, and lightly fry cinnamon and cardamom for 1 minute. Add sliced onions and stir-fry till light brown before adding chicken. Stir ingredients for 10 minutes, then lower heat, cover the pan and allow to simmer.

When chicken is half-cooked, spread green chillies on top so that chicken is completely covered. Sprinkle lemon juice over chillies. Cover the pan again and cook over very low heat till chicken is tender. Remove from heat when very little gravy remains. Serve chicken with chillies on top. Serve with rice or *chapati.*

Chicken Malad

Baking   : 20 mins.
Oven setting: 205°C, 400°F, Gas Regulo 8
Serves   : 6

1 chicken, about 2 pounds (900 g)
2 teaspoons ginger juice
2 teaspoons ground turmeric
salt to taste
¼ cup ghee *or* oil
4 cloves garlic, chopped
4 onions, sliced
1 teaspoon sugar
2 teaspoons ground chilli
1 tablespoon tomato puree
3 eggs, beaten
2 tablespoons cornflour
½ cup cream
2 teaspoons ground black pepper
4 red chillies, sliced
3 teaspoons chopped coriander leaves

Cut chicken into 8 pieces, wash and season with a mixture of ginger juice, vinegar, ground turmeric and salt.

Heat ghee in a pan over medium heat and fry garlic, onions and sugar till brown. Add chicken and ground chilli. Stir-fry for 20 minutes. Pour in tomato puree and 1 cup cold water. Stir to mix well, then lower heat and simmer covered till chicken is tender and very little gravy remains. Remove pan from heat.

In a bowl, mix beaten eggs, cornflour, cream, black pepper and salt. Beat well. Spread chicken curry in a casserole. Pour egg mixture evenly on top and sprinkle with sliced chillies and chopped coriander leaves. Bake for 20 minutes in a moderately hot oven and serve with rice or bread.

Parsi Chicken Roast

Baking   : *30 mins.*
Oven setting: 205°C, 400°F, Gas Regulo 8
Serves   : *6*

1 chicken, about 2 pounds (900 g)
salt to taste
2 cups coconut milk from 1 pound grated coconut
1 stalk lemon grass, crushed
4 red chillies
6 cloves garlic
2 inch (5 cm) piece ginger
a few drops of yellow food colouring
1 tablespoon tomato puree
2 teaspoons honey
a little butter
2 onions, cut into rings
2 teaspoons lemon juice

Clean chicken and cut lengthwise into two (from the neck down). Rub with salt and let stand for 2 hours. Then simmer in coconut milk and lemon grass till chicken is tender and no liquid remains. Remove from heat.

Grind chillies, garlic and ginger together. Mix these with yellow food colouring, tomato puree and honey. Apply this mixture all over the two chicken halves. Grease a baking tray (with butter) and bake chicken in a moderate oven with onion rings on top for 30 minutes till golden brown. Sprinkle lemon juice all over the chicken just before serving.

Dried Chilli Chicken

Serves : 6

1 chicken, about 3 pounds (1350 g)
¼ pound (110 g) dried chillies
1 cup oil
5 cloves, garlic, sliced
2 onions, sliced
¼ cup yoghurt
2 teaspoons ground ginger
1 stalk lemon grass, crushed
1 tablespoon soy sauce
1 teaspoon sugar
salt to taste
3 tomatoes, sliced
2 teaspoons lemon juice

Cut chicken into bite-sized pieces. Remove stems from dried chillies, wash and dry them carefully with a clean tea towel. Heat 3 tablespoons oil in a pan and fry sliced garlic and onions till brown. Add chicken, yoghurt, ginger, lemon grass, soy sauce, sugar and salt. Cover the pan, keep heat low and stir occasionally. Add a little water, if necessary.

In another pan, heat remaining oil over medium heat and fry dried chillies till puffy and dark brown. When chicken is cooked and tender, add fried chillies and tomatoes. When gravy is thick, add lemon juice and remove from heat. Serve chicken with chillies on top. Serve with *chapati* or rice.

Chicken Musallam

Serves : 8

1 chicken, about 3 pounds (1350 g)
½ cup yoghurt
½ tablespoon ginger juice
1 tablespoon ground chilli
2 teaspoons ground coriander
2 teaspoons ground turmeric
1 teaspoon sugar
salt to taste
3 tablespoons melted ghee *or* oil
2 sticks cinnamon
4 pods cardamom
3 onions, sliced
5 cloves garlic, chopped
½ cup cream
¼ pound (110 g) almonds, ground

Clean chicken and cut into 8 pieces. Marinate the pieces in mixture of yoghurt, ginger juice, ground chilli, ground coriander, ground turmeric, sugar and salt for 4 hours.

Heat 2 tablespoons ghee or oil in a pan over medium heat and fry cinnamon and cardamom for 1 minute. Add sliced onions and chopped garlic and stir-fry till slightly brown. Add chicken and lower heat. Cover the pan and simmer, stirring occasionally till liquid has dried up. Add 1 cup boiling hot water and continue simmering if chicken is not quite cooked. When chicken is almost cooked, add beaten cream, stir and cover the pan again, simmering till chicken is cooked.

Heat remaining ghee in a clean pan and fry ground almonds till light brown. Stir this into cooked chicken. Remove pan from heat and serve with fried potatoes and fresh tomatoes.

Kashmiri Chicken Roast

Serves : 6

1 chicken, about 2¾ pounds (1240 g)
2 teaspoons salt
1 teaspoon sugar
juice of ½ lemon
1 teaspoon cardamom
4 cloves
1 teaspoon black peppercorns
¼ cup skinned almonds
¼ cup raisins
2 teaspoons finely chopped ginger
1 teaspoon ground chilli
1 drop red colouring
2 tablespoons butter
1 large onion, chopped
1 cup double cream milk

Skin chicken and prick all over with a fork. Rub with salt, sugar and lemon juice. Set aside.

Grind cardamom, cloves, peppercorns, almonds and raisins together till smooth. Mix ground ingredients with ginger, chilli, red colouring and half the butter. Cream to a smooth paste. Rub butter paste all over chicken and place in a roasting tray. Roast for about 20 minutes.

Melt remaining butter in a pan and fry chopped onions till golden brown. Remove pan from heat, add double cream and stir till it turns yellow. Pour cream over cooked chicken.

75

Chicken in Yoghurt

Serves : 8

8 large pieces of chicken joints
¼ cup melted butter *or* oil *or* ghee
2 onions, sliced
4 cloves garlic, ground
2 teaspoons ground ginger
2 teaspoons ground turmeric
, 4 red chillies, chopped
1 teaspoon sugar
salt to taste
16 cashew-nuts, roasted and ground
½ cup yoghurt
1 teaspoon *garam masala*
2 teaspoons chopped coriander leaves
2 tomatoes, sliced

Wash and dry chicken pieces. Heat butter, oil or ghee in a pan over medium heat. Fry onion, garlic, ginger, ground turmeric, chillies, sugar and salt till light brown. Add chicken pieces and stir till chicken turns golden, then add ground cashew-nuts. Stir to mix and pour in 2 cups water. When it comes to a boil, cover the pan and lower heat.

When chicken is tender, add yoghurt, *garam masala,* chopped coriander leaves and tomato slices. Stir well and simmer for a further 10 minutes before removing from heat. Serve with any salad, bread or rice.

Chicken Doh Piazi

Serves : 8

1 chicken, about 3 pounds (1350 g)
2 teaspoons honey
salt to taste
1 tablespoon vinegar
a few drops of yellow food colouring
6 cloves garlic, ground
2 teaspoons ground ginger
4 tablespoons melted ghee *or* oil
8 onions, sliced
½ teaspoon black cummin
1 tablespoon ground chilli
½ tablespoon ground coriander
½ cup yoghurt
1 teaspoon sugar
1 tablespoon tomato puree

Cut chicken into big pieces, wash, dry with a clean tea towel and rub with a mixture of honey, salt, vinegar and yellow food colouring. Allow to marinate for 2 hours. Mix ground garlic and ginger in ½ cup water. Set aside.

Heat 2 tablespoons melted ghee or oil in a pan over medium heat and fry half the quantity of sliced onions till brown. Remove from oil to a dish. Reheat the oil (if necessary, add more oil) and fry chicken pieces till both sides are brown. Remove from oil and set aside.

In a clean pan, heat another 2 table-spoons oil over medium heat and fry black cummin and 2 tablespoons sliced onions for 10 minutes. Add ½ cup water, ground chilli, ground coriander, yoghurt, sugar and salt to taste. Stir till gravy is dry, then add fried chicken pieces and stir to mix well. Pour in 2 cups water, lower heat and cover the pan to simmer. When chicken is tender and gravy has thickened, add remaining sliced onions, tomato puree and the ginger and garlic mixture. Stir for about 20 minutes. Add fried onions and remove from heat.

Butter Chicken

Serves : 6

1 chicken, about 2 pounds (900 g)
salt to taste
2 cups coconut milk from ½ pound (225 g) grated
   coconut
5 tablespoons melted butter
4 cloves garlic, chopped
4 onions, sliced
2 teaspoons ground chilli
2 teaspoons ginger juice
3 red chillies, halved

Tomato cream sauce

1 tablespoon melted butter
1 teaspoon shredded ginger
5 tomatoes, chopped
1 teaspoon ground chilli
2 teaspoons salt
1 teaspoon sugar
2 teaspoons cornflour
2 tablespoons thick cream
1 tablespoon tomato puree
2 teaspoons chopped coriander leaves
2 teaspoons lemon juice
1 teaspoon *garam masala*

Cut chicken into 8 pieces, wash and bring to a boil with salt and coconut milk. Lower heat, cover the pan and simmer till chicken is tender and almost dry. Remove from heat.

In a pan, heat 4 tablespoons butter over medium heat and fry chopped garlic and sliced onions for 5 minutes, then add boiled chicken, ground chilli and ginger juice. Stir-fry for 10 minutes. Add tomato cream sauce (see below) and sliced chillies. Stir well, remove from heat and pour 1 tablespoon melted butter over chicken. Serve with *chapati* or rice.

Tomato cream sauce

Heat butter in a small pan over low heat and add ginger, tomatoes, ground chilli, salt and sugar. Cook for 5 minutes. Beat cornflour and cream with a little water and mix with tomato puree. Add to contents of the pan and cook till sauce thickens. Then remove from heat and stir in chopped coriander leaves, lemon juice and *garam masala*. Keep covered till needed.

Chutneys, Pickles and Salads

Sweet Mango Pickle

10 unripe mangoes
salt to taste
6 cloves garlic, sliced
2 teaspoons ground turmeric
3 pounds (1350 g) sugar
1 tablespoon roasted ground sweet cummin
1 tablespoon ground mustard seed
3 teaspoons ground chilli
½ cup vinegar

Peel mangoes and halve them lengthwise, then cut each half into 4 pieces. You would get 8 pieces for each mango. Discard the seed. Wash mangoes and rub with salt, garlic and ground turmeric. Leave in the sun for 2 or 3 days.

Boil sugar with 1 cup water till syrup is thick and sticky, then remove from heat and cool. Put mangoes into the syrup, followed by ground spices and vinegar. Stir to mix. Transfer the mixture into a few glass jars and leave them in the sun for 3 or 4 days. Turn the mixture thoroughly once more and again sun for 3 or 4 days. The pickle can be stored for about 6 months if kept in a cool place.

Grated Mango Pickle

10 unripe mangoes
2 teaspoons salt
2 teaspoons ground chilli
2 teaspoons ground turmeric
2 pounds (900 g) sugar
1 teaspoon ground mustard seed
2 teaspoons roasted ground sweet cummin
1 tablespoon mustard oil *or* olive oil

Peel mangoes, wash and grate flesh very finely. Add salt, ground chilli and ground turmeric. Mix well and sun the mixture for 3 or 4 days till it is soft. When it is very soft, add sugar, ground mustard, ground sweet cummin and oil. Mix thoroughly and leave the mixture spread out on a tray in the sun for another 3 or 4 days. When it is well dried, store in a glass jar. This pickle will keep for a year.

Sour Mango Pickle

10 unripe mangoes
1 tablespoon salt
2 tablespoons sugar
2 teaspoons ground turmeric
1 tablespoon mustard seed
3 teaspoons sweet cummin
2 teaspoons fenugreek
1 tablespoon mustard oil *or* olive oil

Leave the skin of mangoes on. Wash and halve lengthwise. Remove the seed. Dissolve salt and sugar in 1 cup water and fill the hollows of mango halves with this solution. Sun for 2 days, then drain the solution into a bowl.

Grind all ingredients except mangoes and oil and mix ground ingredients with the solution taken from the mango hollows. Heat oil in a pan over medium heat and fry the spices for 10 minutes or till the raw smell goes. Stir continuously. Remove from heat and allow to cool. Put the fried ingredients into the hollow part of the mangoes and sun every day till mangoes are soft. The pickle may be stored for about 4 months if kept in a cool place in glass jars.

Mango Sambal

5 unripe mangoes
3 red chillies
2 shallots
1 teaspoon chopped ginger
2 teaspoons chopped coriander leaves
2 teaspoons salt
3 tablespoons sugar

Peel mangoes and cut flesh into small pieces. Grind or pound them with chillies, shallots, chopped ginger and coriander leaves. Stir in salt and sugar, store in a glass jar and keep in a cool place. This sambal goes particularly well with fish curries.

Lime or Lemon Pickle

1 pound (450 g) green or slightly yellow
   limes *or* lemons
1 cup mustard oil *or* olive oil
1 tablespoon sweet cummin
2 teaspoons black cummin
2 or 3 red chillies, halved
1½ tablespoons salt
2 teaspoons ground chilli
1 tablespoon ground mustard seed

Cut limes or lemons into small cubes. Remove all pips, taking care to catch juice in a bowl.

Heat 1 tablespoon oil and fry sweet cummin, black cummin, chillies and salt.

Stir and simmer for a minute or two. Remove from heat and stir in ground chilli.

Mix the fried ingredients with fruit. Shake well, store in earthenware or glass jars and keep in a warm cupboard for a week. Shake the jars every day and, if possible, sun them for 2 or 3 hours a day. At the end of a week, stir in ground mustard and the rest of the oil so that the pickle is really saturated with oil. More oil can be added, if necessary. Pickle may be stored for 1 year.

Tomato Bhurta

6 ripe tomatoes
1 onion
2 green chillies
3 teaspoons sugar
salt to taste
2 teaspoons lime juice

Fully immerse tomatoes in boiling water for 30 seconds to loosen the skin, then dip in cold water. When cool enough to handle, peel off the skin. Halve the tomatoes widthwise (not through the stem) and press gently to extrude the seeds. Mash the pulp which remains with a fork, discarding any hard parts.

Chop onion and green chillies very finely and mix with tomato pulp. Add sugar, salt and lime juice. Stir to mix thoroughly and set aside in a cool place.

Eggplant Bhurta

1 pound (450 g) eggplants
2 teaspoons oil
1 onion
2 green chillies
1 ounce (30 g) ghee *or* butter
salt to taste
½ teaspoon sugar
2 teaspoons chopped coriander leaves

Rub eggplants all over with oil and put under a grill. Grill slowly, turning from side to side for about 20 minutes till the skin is scorched black and pulp inside is soft. Peel and mash the pulp with a fork.

Chop onion and chillies. Heat ghee or butter in a pan over medium heat and lightly brown chopped onion. Add chopped chillies and eggplant pulp. Stir-fry for a few minutes, then add salt, sugar, chopped coriander leaves. Stir well and remove from heat.

Onion Salad

½ pound (225 g) onions
1 tomato
2 small cucumbers
2 green chillies
2 teaspoons lemon juice
1 teaspoon sugar
1 teaspoon salt
2 teaspoons chopped coriander leaves

Peel and cut onions into very thin rings. Peel and chop tomato and cucumbers.

(See Tomato Bhurta above for the method of peeling a tomato and removing the seeds.)

Halve green chillies lengthwise (from the stem) and scrape out the seeds. Chop finely. Mix lemon juice, sugar and salt in a cup. Toss onion, cucumber and chilli together in a glass dish and sprinkle lemon juice over these. Refrigerate. Mix in chopped tomato and sprinkle chopped coriander leaves on top just before serving.

Cucumber Raita

2 cups yoghurt
2 large cucumbers
2 green chillies
2 teaspoons butter
½ teaspoon mustard seed
1 onion, cut into very thin rings
2 tomatoes, sliced
1 tablespoon cooked green peas
2 teaspoons roasted ground cummin
2 teaspoons lime *or* lemon juice
1 teaspoon sugar
salt to taste

Put yoghurt in a bowl and beat with a fork till smooth and thick, like a paste. Peel and grate cucumber. Halve the chillies lengthwise and discard seeds, then chop finely.

Heat butter in a pan and fry mustard seed till you hear a popping sound. Add mustard seed and all other ingredients to yoghurt. Stir well and refrigerate. Serve cold. This relish is especially good with *pillaus.*

Sweet Mango Chutney

10 unripe mangoes
4 or 5 dried chillies
1 tablespoon oil
2 teaspoons *panch masala*
2 inch (5 cm) piece ginger, very thinly sliced
2 teaspoons chopped raisins
1 tablespoon vinegar
2 teaspoons ground turmeric
2 pounds (900 g) sugar
salt to taste
2 teaspoons ground mustard seed
2 teaspoons roasted ground sweet cummin

Heat oil in a *wok* over medium heat and fry dried chillies till dark brown and puffy. Add *panch masala,* ginger and chopped raisins. Stir-fry for 5 minutes. Add mangoes together with vinegar, ground turmeric, sugar and salt. Fry till sugar is brown and mangoes are soft. Remove pan from heat and mix in ground mustard and sweet cummin.

Peel mangoes and halve them lengthwise, then cut each half into 4. Discard seeds, wash and dry. Pluck out the stems of dried chillies.

Tomato Chutney

1 pound (450 g) large, ripe tomatoes
2 teaspoons oil
½ teaspoon sweet cummin
3 dried chillies
1 teaspoon chopped ginger
4 teaspoons raisins
salt to taste
4 tablespoons sugar
2 tablespoons lemon juice
2 tablespoons tomato puree
2 teaspoons roasted ground sweet cummin

Dip tomatoes into boiling water for 30 seconds to loosen the skin. then cool in cold water and peel off the skin. Quarter each tomato.

Heat oil in a pan over medium heat and stir-fry sweet cummin, chillies, ginger and raisins for 5 minutes. Add tomatoes, salt, sugar, lemon juice and tomato puree. Stir continuously till the chutney thickens. Turn the heat down to very low as it becomes thicker. It should be almost as thick as honey when cold. Add roasted ground sweet cummin, stir well and remove from heat. Allow to cool, bottle and keep refrigerated. Tomato chutney can be kept refrigerated for months. Serve with *pillau* or *loochi*.

Prune, Date and Raisin Chutney

¼ pound (110 g) seedless dried prunes
¼ pound (110 g) seedless dates
¼ pound (110 g) raisins
½ cup tamarind
3 teaspoons cooking oil
4 dried chillies
1 teaspoon mustard seed
2 teaspoons chopped ginger
salt to taste
1 cup sugar
4 red chillies
2 teaspoons roasted ground sweet cummin

Soak prunes and dates in cold water for about 2 hours to soften. Grind the raisins. Cover the tamarind in water, then work with your fingers, kneading and mashing pulp, to remove the seeds.

Run tamarind through a strainer into a bowl. Press in a circular motion downwards to ensure that all the soft pulp goes through. Make sure you scrape the other side of the strainer as it tends to cling. Discard seeds and hard skin.

Heat oil in a pan over medium heat and stir-fry dried chillies, mustard seed and chopped ginger till chillies are puffy and dark brown. Add softened prunes, dates, ground raisins, tamarind pulp, salt, sugar and ½ cup water to help cook the ingredients.

Stir continuously till gravy thickens, then lower heat and continue stirring. When gravy is very thick, add red chillies and ground sweet cummin. Simmer for another 10 minutes, then remove from heat. Keep chutney in the freezer (may be stored for 2 weeks) and serve with *chapati,* rice or bread.

(clockwise) — Orange Cups, Channa Jilapi, Channa Chom Chom
(Recipes: pp. 105, 96)

Top — Rossogolla (left)
Boondi (right)
Bottom — Channa Sandesh
(Recipes: pp. 90, 102, 92)

Top — Vegetable Khitchri
Bottom — Lemon Pickle
(surrounding the dishes are Papadums, crackers commonly eaten with Indian food)
(Recipes: pp. 6, 79)

Left — Tandoori Chicken
Right — Naan
(Recipes: pp. 69, 16)

Fresh Apple Chutney

4 green apples, not too ripe
2 ounces (60 g) finely ground coconut
2 onions, finely chopped
2 red chillies, chopped
4 teaspoons sugar
salt to taste
2 teaspoons lemon juice

Cook apples by boiling. Then peel, core and dice them. Soak in cold salt water for 30 minutes. Then drain and mix with the other ingredients. Put into an attractive glass dish, sprinkle lemon juice over the chutney and refrigerate.

Padina (Mint) Chutney (1)

10 sprigs mint
1 onion
2 red chillies
1 inch (2½ cm) piece ginger
2 teaspoons sugar
salt to taste
6 ounces (180 g) yoghurt
2 teaspoons lemon juice

Chop mint, onion, chillies and ginger. Put these and other ingredients in an electric blender and blend at high speed for a few minutes. Keep in glass jars and refrigerate. This chutney goes well with *kababs* and can be stored for 2 weeks.

Padina (Mint) Chutney (2)

¼ cup (packed) mint leaves
2 shallots
1 inch (2½ cm) piece ginger
2 green chillies
½ tablespoon pomegranate seeds or *anardana* (available dried at Indian grocers)
6 teaspoons lemon or tamarind juice
2 tablespoons sugar
salt to taste

Chop mint leaves, shallots, ginger and green chillies. Grind these and pomegranate seeds together. Add lemon juice, sugar and salt and mix well. Refrigerate and serve in a glass dish. Mint chutney will keep for a few days, if refrigerated. Serve with *paratha* and any fried dish.

Imli (Tamarind) Chutney

¼ pound (110 g) tamarind
3 teaspoons ground raisins
2 teaspoons roasted ground chilli
1 teaspoon roasted ground sweet cummin
1 teaspoon ground mustard seed
2 pounds sugar
salt to taste

Soak tamarind in ¾ cup water for 30 minutes, then rub well with your fingers to mash the pulp and separate it from the seeds. Put this through a strainer. Press down so that all the pulp goes through. Be sure to scrape the pulp which will cling to the underside of the strainer into the bowl. Discard seeds and skin.

Add the other ingredients to tamarind pulp and mix thoroughly. Simmer over low heat till dry. Your chutney is now ready for refrigeration. Serve cold in a non-metallic dish with any Indian savoury. If chutney is kept in glass jars and left in the sun for 1-2 days, it may be stored for about 1 year.

Pineapple Chutney

Serves : 10

1 big cooking pineapple
3 teaspoons oil
4 dried chillies
½ teaspoon mustard seed
1 tablespoon raisins
1 teaspoon ground turmeric
2 tablespoons lemon juice
1 teaspoon salt
¼ cup sugar
2 teaspoons plain white flour
3 green chillies, halved

Cut off the skin and remove the "eyes" of the pineapple. Halve it lengthwise and grate in a circular motion till you reach the core of the pineapple. Discard this.

Heat oil in a pan over medium heat and stir-fry dried chillies and mustard seed till chillies are dark brown and puffy. Add grated pineapple, raisins, ground turmeric, lemon juice, salt and sugar. Bring to a gentle boil, then lower heat and continue cooking, stirring all the while. Mix flour with a little water and stir into pineapple mixture. When mixture is quite thick, add green chillies and remove from heat. It will keep for weeks refrigerated. Serve cold.

Desserts

Bread Raitha

Serves: 8

1 pound (450 g) bread slices
¼ cup ghee
1½ cups yoghurt
1 tablespoon sugar
1 teaspoon salt
2 teaspoons roasted ground chilli
1 teaspoon mustard seed
2 teaspoons melted butter
2 teaspoons lemon juice
1 teaspoon finely chopped coriander leaves
2 red chillies, finely chopped

Cut off crusts of bread and halve the slices. Heat 2 teaspoons ghee in a frying pan over low heat. Swirl the pan around a couple of times to coat the bottom of the pan with oil. Fry 2 or 3 slices of bread till light brown. Continue frying bread slices, a few at a time, adding a little ghee for each lot of slices. Cool and cut into 1 inch (2½ cm) squares. Arrange in a flat dish.

Beat yoghurt, sugar, salt and ground chilli with a fork till a smooth paste is obtained. Pour this mixture over the bread squares.

Fry mustard seed in hot butter till they pop. Sprinkle mustard seed, lemon juice, chopped coriander leaves and chopped red chillies over the bread and yoghurt. Serve with rice.

Bread Shahi Tookri

Serves : 8

1 pound (450 g) bread slices
¼ cup ghee
10 cups milk
½ cup sugar
1 teaspoon ground cardamom
3 teaspoons raisins
3 teaspoons chopped pistachios
3 teaspoons chopped almonds

Cut off crust of bread. Fry bread slices in the way described for Bread Raitha and cut into 1 inch (2½ cm) squares.

Bring milk to a boil on medium heat, then turn down heat and simmer, stirring continuously till liquid is reduced by half. Add sugar and ground cardamom. Stir for a few minutes and remove from heat.

Arrange bread squares in a pie dish and pour thick milk over bread. Sprinkle with raisins, pistachios and almonds and serve cool.

Rossogolla

Serves : 8

2 pounds (900 g) sugar
6 cups water
2 pounds (900 g) *channa*
4 teaspoons ghee
2 teaspoons ground semolina
½ teaspoon ground cardamom
2 teaspoons plain white flour
a few drops of rose essence *or* any other essence
  preferred

First prepare the syrup. Put sugar and water in a saucepan and boil for 20-30 minutes to get a thick syrup. In the meantime, prepare the *channa* balls.

Put channa, ghee, semolina, cardamom and flour in a bowl and work with the fingers till mixture is creamy and smooth.

Shape into balls of 1½ inch (4 cm) diameter and gently drop them into the boiling syrup. Simmer *channa* balls in syrup for about 25 minutes. The balls will expand and become spongy. Turn off heat and after about 10 minutes, add rose essence. Cool the balls in syrup and leave at room temperature. When serving, place a few rossogolla in small dishes with a little syrup. Only the rossogolla should be eaten, not the syrup.

Rossomalai

Serves : 8

2 ½ pounds (1125 g) sugar
8 cups water
1 pound (450 g) *channa*
4 teaspoons ghee
2 teaspoons plain white flour
3 teaspoons fine semolina
1 teaspoon ground cardamom (skinned)
a few small pieces rock sugar (the size of peanuts)
a few drops of red food colouring
6 cups milk
2 teaspoons chopped almonds
2 teaspoons chopped pistachios
1 teaspoon roasted ground cardamom

Get the syrup ready first. Boil 2 pounds (900 g) sugar in 4 cups water for about 20 minutes, then lower heat. While syrup is simmering, mix *channa,* ghee, flour, semolina and cardamom in a bowl. Work thoroughly with the fingers and heel of palm to get a really smooth mixture.

In another small bowl, mix rock sugar with red colouring till all the pieces are coated with it. Shape *channa* mixture into balls of 1 ½ inch (4 cm) diameter. Make a hollow in the centre, drop in a piece of coloured rock sugar and pat into a round shape again. Drop gently into simmering syrup and cook for 40 minutes. Then remove from heat and allow to cool for at least 20 minutes. Drain well.

In another saucepan, bring milk to a boil. Lower heat, add ½ pound (225 g) sugar and simmer for 50 minutes till milk is reduced to half its original volume. Add chopped nuts and rossomalai, and simmer for another 10 minutes. Turn off heat and sprinkle roasted ground cardamom over rossomalai. Chill in the refrigerator overnight before serving with thick milk.

Steamed Yoghurt

Baking   : 30 mins.
Oven setting : 110°C, 225°F, Gas Regulo 1
Serves   : 6

4 cups milk (evaporated)
¼ cup sugar
½ teaspoon ground cardamom (skinned)
2 cups yoghurt
12 seeds pistachios, chopped

Bring milk to a boil, then turn down heat to low and simmer, stirring continuously, till milk is reduced to half the original quantity. Mix in sugar, pistachio and ground cardamom. Set aside for about 20 minutes to cool.

Beat yoghurt with a fork till quite smooth. Stir into milk and pour the mixture into a heatproof shallow dish. Steam over vigorously boiling water to bake in a moderately hot oven for 30 minutes or till it hardens. Chill in the refrigerator before serving.

Mulpua

Serves : 6

1 cup full-cream milk powder
¼ cup plain white flour
1 tablespoon fine semolina
½ teaspoon baking powder
1 tablespoon melted ghee
2 teaspoons chopped almonds
3 teaspoons raisins
½ teaspoon sweet cummin
2 pounds (900 g) sugar
6 cups water
6 tablespoons ghee or oil for frying

Put milk powder in a bowl. Sift flour, semolina and baking powder into the same bowl. Rub in melted ghee and add a little water at a time, stirring all the while to get a smooth, thick batter with a pouring consistency. Add almonds, raisins and sweet cummin. Whisk for 10 minutes.

Make the syrup by boiling sugar in 6 cups water till sugar dissolves and mixture is thick. Pour syrup into a large serving bowl.

Heat 6 tablespoons ghee or oil in a frying pan over medium heat. Pour in ½ tablespoon batter to make a small pancake. You can make 2 at a time. Fry till brown. If it browns too quickly, adjust heat. Remove from pan when golden brown and drop into the warm syrup. Continue frying till all the batter is used up. More oil will have to be added after every 2 or 3 lots of pancakes. Mulpua should be served when cooled.

Channa Sandesh

Serves : 8

1 pound (450 g) *channa*
3 teaspoons plain flour
¼ cup condensed milk
1 tablespoon full-cream milk powder
½ pound (225 g) sugar
3 teaspoons chopped almonds
3 teaspoons chopped pistachios
1 teaspoon ground cardamom (skinned)

Put all ingredients, except pistachios and cardamom, in a bowl and knead well for 10 minutes. Heat a saucepan and put in the mixture. Cook over low heat for 30 minutes until dry. Remove pan from heat, add pistachios and cardamom and mix well. When cool enough to handle, mould into various flat shapes and cool before serving.

Dom Sandesh

Serves : 8

1 pound (450 g) *channa*
20 almonds, chopped
½ cup condensed milk
¼ pound (110 g) sugar
1 teaspoon roasted ground cardamom (skinned)
¼ pound (110 g) *khoa*
1 teaspoon chopped pistachios

Mix *channa* with chopped almonds, condensed milk and sugar. If the *channa* is made from milk powder, add 1 tablespoon full-cream milk powder. Put the mixture into a saucepan and cook for 30 minutes on low heat, stirring until dry.

In a clean, dry saucepan, fry *khoa* on very low heat till it is quite dry. It will be a light brown and sticky solid. Cool for 2 hours, then mix with chopped pistachios and ¼ teaspoon ground cardamom.

Mould *channa* mixture into balls of about 1½ inch (4 cm) diameter, place 1½ teaspoons *khoa* mixture in the centre and pat into flat shapes, or mould into any shape desired.

Steamed Curd Sandesh

Baking : 20 mins.
Oven setting : 150°C, 300°F, Gas Regulo 4
Serves : 8

½ cup *channa*
½ cup thick milk *or* condensed milk
¼ cup yoghurt
1 tablespoon full-cream milk powder
2 teaspoons plain flour
2 teaspoons ghee
2 teaspoons chopped almonds
1 teaspoon ground cardamom (skinned)
2 teaspoons chopped pistachios
extra sugar for sprinkling
sugar to taste

Mix *channa* with all ingredients except pistachios in a bowl. Beat well with a wooden spoon for 10 minutes, then pour into a heat-proof dish and steam over vigorously boiling water for minutes, until mixture hardens.

Remove from steamer, sprinkle chopped pistachios and a little sugar on top and bake in a moderately hot oven for 20 minutes. Remove from the oven, allow to cool, then cut into squares to serve.

Pantua or Gulab Jamun

Serves : 8

3 pounds (1350 g) sugar
5 cups water
1 tablespoon plain white flour
¼ teaspoon baking powder
2 teaspoons fine semolina
1 teaspoon ground cardamom (skinned)
½ pound (225 g) *channa*
½ pound (225 g) *khoa*
1 tablespoon melted ghee
ghee for deep-fat frying
a few drops of rose essence

First make the syrup by boiling sugar in water till all sugar dissolves and a fairly thick mixture is obtained. Turn off heat and pour half the syrup into a saucepan. Put the rest in a serving bowl.

Sift flour, baking powder and semolina into a bowl. Add ground cardamom. Mix well, then rub in *channa, khoa* and melted ghee. Work with the fingers and heel of the palm till a smooth pliable dough is obtained. Mould into small balls of 1 inch (2½ cm) diameter or cigar-like shapes about 2 inches (5 cm) long.

Heat ghee in a deep pan over low heat. At the same time, bring syrup in the saucepan to a boil and remove from heat. Fry pantua a few at a time on low heat till dark brown. They should take about 10 minutes to brown. If they brown too quickly, adjust heat. Remove and drop into simmering syrup.

Add a few drops of rose essence and cool in the refrigerator for a day before serving. Pantua will keep for a few weeks refrigerated and immersed in syrup. Serve from the bowl but take only the pantua, not the syrup, when eating.

Besan Laddu

1 cup horsegram *dhal* **flour (besan), sifted**
¼ cup ghee
1 teaspoon black pepper
1 teaspoon ground cardamom
2 teaspoons chopped pistachio
¾ cup castor sugar
a little milk, if necessary

Stir-fry *dhal* flour with ghee over low heat till golden brown. Stir in pepper, cardamom and pistachio. Remove from heat.

Rub in castor sugar thoroughly and mould into small balls while still hot. A little milk may be added if mixture is too dry.

Besan laddu balls can be kept refrigerated for as long as 2 weeks.

Cashew-nut Laddu

1 cup roasted cashew-nuts
1 cup sugar
½ cup cold water
1 tablespoon condensed milk
1 teaspoon cardamom
1 tablespoon fried raisins
2 teaspoons finely chopped pistachios

Grind roasted cashew-nuts to a crumbly powder.

Boil sugar with water till a thick syrup is obtained. Add milk, cardamom and raisins. Add three-quarters of the ground cashew-nuts and stir to a thick paste. Mould into small balls.

Mix remaining ground cashew-nuts with chopped pistachio in a bowl. Coat balls one by one with this mixture.

Laddu can be kept refrigerated for 2 weeks.

Raj Bhog

Serves : 6

2 pounds (900 g) *channa*
4 teaspoons ghee
2 teaspoons fine semolina
2 teaspoons plain white flour
¼ teaspoon baking powder
1 teaspoon ground cardamom (skinned)
¼ pound (110 g) *khoa*
2 teaspoons chopped pistachios
2 pounds (900 g) sugar
a few drops of red food colouring
6 cups water
2 tablespoons sugar for sprinkling

Mix *channa,* ghee, semolina, flour, baking powder and cardamom in a bowl and knead well till smooth and soft. Divide *khoa* into lumps the size of small marbles and put a little chopped pistachio and sugar, coloured red, in the centre.

Shape *channa* mixture into 2 inch (5 cm) balls. Make a hollow in the centre and put in *khoa* ball. Mould back into a round ball, covering the hollow.

While preparing raj bhog, boil sugar in 6 cups water till all sugar dissolves. Gently drop raj bhog into syrup and boil gently over low heat for 50 minutes, then sprinkle 2 tablespoons sugar over it. Cover pan and simmer on low heat till raj bhog sinks. Remove from heat and allow to cool to room temperature.

Channa Jilapi

Serves : 8

1 pound (450 g) *channa*
½ pound (225 g) ghee
3 tablespoons plain white flour
½ teaspoon baking powder
2 teaspoons rice flour
1 teaspoon ground cardamom (skinned)
⅓ teaspoon saffron
1 tablespoon water
2½ pounds (1125 g) sugar
6 cups water
2 tablespoons full-cream milk powder

Mix *channa* with 2 tablespoons ghee in a bowl. Sift in plain flour, baking powder, milk powder and rice flour. Add cardamom and saffron and 1 tablespoon water. Knead for 10 minutes to obtain a soft pasty dough. Divide dough into

lumps the size of tennis balls. Put a lump into an icing bag with a ¼ inch (½ cm) plain nozzle. Pipe onto a lightly floured tray in a circular motion. Begin with a circle of about 4 inch (10 cm) diameter and pipe inwards till you reach the centre. The figure would be like a mosquito coil.

When all the lumps have been piped into coils, heat a saucepan and boil sugar and 6 cups water till sugar dissolves and a thick mixture is obtained. Turn off heat.

Heat remaining ghee in a *wok* or deep frying pan over low heat and fry jilapi 4 or 6 at a time till brown. Remove and immerse in warm syrup. Serve when cooled to room temperature.

goↄB įɒЯ

Channa Chom Chom

Serves : 8

2 pounds (900 g) sugar
6 cups water
1 pound (450 g) *channa*
4 teaspoons ghee
3 teaspoons fine semolina
2 teaspoons plain white flour
¼ teaspoon baking powder
1 teaspoon ground cardamom (skinned)
¼ pound (110 g) *khoa*
2 tablespoons sugar

Put sugar and 6 cups water in a saucepan and boil till sugar dissolves. Mix *channa* with ghee, semolina, flour, baking powder and cardamom in a bowl. Press against the side

of the bowl till quite smooth, then mould into flat oval shapes of about 2 inches (5 cm) in diameter. Boil chom chom in syrup for 50 minutes. Sprinkle 2 tablespoons sugar all over chom chom and cover the pan. Simmer on low heat till chom chom sink in the syrup, then remove from heat.

In a clean, dry pan, stir-fry *khoa,* on very low heat until dry. Leave aside for 2 hours to cool, then grind or pound coarsely.

Leave chom chom to cool for one day in the syrup. Drain the syrup well. To serve, coat chom chom with ground khoa.

Vermicelli Kheer

Serves : 8

1 ounce (30 g) ghee
4 ounces (110 g) fine vermicelli
10 cups milk
3 bay leaves
6 ounces (180 g) sugar
1 ounce (30 g) raisins
1 ounce (30 g) chopped almonds
1 teaspoon ground cardamom (skinned)
1 tablespoon roasted cashew-nuts
2 teaspoons pistachios

Heat ghee in a pan over medium heat and fry vermicelli till slightly browned. Remove to a dish.

In the same pan, bring milk to a boil with bay leaves. Add sugar and stir till dissolved, then add fried vermicelli, raisins and almonds. Cook slowly till mixture thickens and vermicelli has absorbed most of the milk. Remove from heat and stir in ground cardamom. Pour into a large, glass serving bowl or individual custard bowls and sprinkle cashew-nuts and pistachios on top. Serve at room temperature.

Semolina Kheer

Serves : 10

¼ cup semolina
1 tablespoon ghee
10 cups thin milk
½ cup sugar
3 bay leaves
2 teaspoons chopped almonds
2 tablespoons raisins
½ teaspoon saffron
1 teaspoon ground cardamom (skinned)

As in the case of Vermicelli Kheer, fry semolina in ghee till lightly browned.

Remove to a dish and bring milk to a boil with sugar and bay leaves. Add almonds, raisins and saffron and simmer till mixture thickens. Then remove from heat and stir in ground cardamom. Cool to lukewarm, then refrigerate. Serve chilled with tinned or fresh fruit.

Rice Kheer

Serves : 10

2 tablespoons *Basmati* rice (*or* any good quality
   rice)
3 teaspoons ghee
12 cups milk
3 bay leaves
2 tablespoons raisins
¼ pound (110 g) rock sugar
4 teaspoons chopped almonds
1 teaspoon ground cardamom (skinned)
4 teaspoons chopped pistachio

Wash rice grains, drain water and stir-fry with ghee over medium heat for 10 minutes until light brown. Remove from heat.

Boil milk till it is reduced to about two-thirds the original amount. Add rice, bay leaves and raisins and stir well. When rice is almost cooked, stir in sugar and almonds. After about 10 minutes, add ground cardamom and remove saucepan from heat. Refrigerate and serve cold, garnished with pistachio.

Kheer Kadam

Serves : 10

2 pounds (900 g) *channa*
4 teaspoons ghee
2 teaspoons ground semolina
2 teaspoons plain white flour
a pinch of baking powder
1 teaspoon roasted ground cardamom (skinned)
2 pounds (900 g) sugar
6 cups water
1 pound (450 g) *khoa*

Mix *channa* with ghee, semolina, flour, baking powder and 1 teaspoon ground cardamom. Use a wooden spoon or the heel of the palm to press *channa* against the side of the bowl to make it really smooth. Shape into balls of 1 inch (2 ½ cm) diameter.

Leaving 2 tablespoons sugar for caramel, 1 tablespoon for use later, make a syrup by boiling remaining sugar in 6 cups water till sugar dissolves. Immerse *channa* balls in syrup and boil till brown.

If syrup gets too thick while boiling, add a little boiling water. When *channa* balls sink in syrup, turn heat off and leave in syrup to cool.

In the meantime, put ¾ of the *khoa* in a bowl and stir in ½ teaspoon ground cardamom and 1 tablespoon sugar. Fry the remaining *khoa* in a clean, dry pan over medium heat, stirring all the while till *khoa* is dry. Grind or pound to a dust.

Soak *channa* balls in the syrup for one day. Drain syrup from *channa* balls and pat on a thick coat of soft *khoa*. Roll in *khoa* dust. Do this for all the *channa* balls. Serve at room temperature. Kheer kadam may be stored in the freezer for 2-3 months.

Kheer Kamala

Serves : 10

6 large seedless oranges
1 tablespoon castor sugar
6 cups milk
¼ pound (110 g) sugar
4 teaspoons finely chopped almonds
a few drops of rose essence

Use a potato peeler to peel one orange very thinly. Cut the peel into fine shreds. Put in a bowl and cover with boiling water. After 20 minutes drain and sprinkle with castor sugar. Put aside. Peel the remaining oranges with a very sharp knife, then cut out the segments of all oranges leaving the membrane and pith behind. Arrange the segments in a serving dish.

Boil milk with ¼ pound (110 g) sugar and chopped almonds on low heat, stirring all the while till milk is reduced to half its original volume. Turn off heat and allow to cool to room temperature, then stir in rose essence and pour over orange segments in the serving dish. Chill and garnish with shreds of candied orange peel before serving.

Monmohini

Serves : 8

½ cup *khoa*
½ cup white grated coconut
2 pounds (900 g) sugar
1 tablespoon plain white flour
2 teaspoons fine semolina
1 teaspoon ground cardamom (skinned)
4 cups water
ghee for frying

Mix *khoa* with grated coconut, flour, semolina and cardamom. Put the mixture in a saucepan and cook, stirring, over very low heat till it is soft and sticky. This should not take more than 40 minutes. Remove from heat and allow to cool. In another saucepan, boil remaining sugar in 4 cups water till sugar dissolves. Remove from heat.

When coconut mixture is cool enough to handle, shape into balls the size of large marbles, then flatten. Heat 3 tablespoons ghee in a pan over medium heat and fry a few monmohini at a time till dark brown. Remove with a slotted spoon and immerse in warm syrup. When serving, take a few monmohini out of the syrup, leaving the rest immersed till ready to serve.

Lalmohon

Serves : 8

2 cups full-cream milk powder
¼ pound (110 g) melted ghee
4 teaspoons castor sugar
¼ teaspoon ground cardamom
4 teaspoons plain white flour
½ teaspoon baking powder
2 teaspoons fine semolina
4 teaspoons granulated sugar
2 drops red food colouring
1½ pounds (675 g) sugar
2 cups water

Put milk powder in a bowl and rub in 6 teaspoons melted ghee. Add castor sugar, ground cardamom, flour, baking powder and semolina. Mix thoroughly, then slowly add a little cold water, a few teaspoonfuls at a time. Mix granulated sugar and red food colouring together in a cup. Make the syrup by boiling 1½ pounds (675 g) sugar in 2 cups water till sugar dissolves.

Divide dough into balls the size of marbles. Make a hollow in the centre and put in a little coloured sugar. Pat back into shape and fry in ghee over very low heat till dark brown. Move the balls in the ghee frequently to prevent burning. When cooked, remove with a slotted spoon and immerse in warm syrup. Serve cool with a few drops of rose essence added, if desired.

Cashew-nut Barfi

Serves : 8

2 pounds (900 g) cashew-nuts
1 cup condensed milk
2 teaspoons plain white flour
ghee *or* butter for greasing tray and knife

Roast cashew-nuts in a clean dry pan over very low heat. Stir frequently, moving the spoon down the side, under the nuts and up the centre so that the nuts are browned evenly. When nuts are light brown, remove and pound coarsely. Put half the pounded nuts in a saucepan and add condensed milk and flour. Mix well and cook over low heat, stirring till it takes on an almost solid consistency. Remove from heat.

Grease a baking tray and spread cooked mixture smoothly and thinly with a greased knife. Sprinkle remaining pounded cashew-nuts evenly over the spread mixture and use the palm of your hand to press it down. Set aside to cool to room temperature, then cut into diamond shapes. Store in a tightly covered jar. Cashew-nut Barfi can be kept for 2 to 3 weeks.

Coconut Barfi

Serves : 8

1 pound (450 g) sugar
½ cup water
1 ½ pounds (675 g) white grated coconut
1 cup full-cream milk powder
¼ teaspoon saffron
1 teaspoon roasted ground cardamom or vanilla for flavour
1 tablespoon chopped pistachios for garnishing
butter for greasing tray and knife

Heat a heavy-bottomed saucepan and boil sugar in water till it dissolves and thickens. Turn heat to low and add grated coconut and milk powder. Stir well and continue cooking on low heat, stirring all the time. When it is done, the mixture should leave the sides of the pan in one mass as you stir. At this stage, add saffron and ground cardamom or vanilla. Stir to mix well, then remove from heat.

Spread the mixture on a greased tray. Use a buttered knife to spread it thinly and smoothen the surface. Press the edge of a knife over the surface to make out diamond shapes, then press a few pistachios in the centre of each shape. When it is lukewarm, cut out the shapes. Separate them when cooled to room temperature.

Kulfi

Serves : 4

2 teaspoons gelatin
2 tablespoons cold water
½ cup evaporated milk
1 egg white, whipped
1 tablespoon sugar
½ tablespoon finely chopped pistachios
½ teaspoon vanilla essence *or* roasted ground cardamom

Chill evaporated milk in the refrigerator for a day before use. This makes milk lighter on beating. Mix gelatin with cold water and heat to dissolve gelatin. Remove from heat and stir in milk. Return to the stove and bring to a boil, then turn off heat and add whipped egg white, sugar, pistachios and flavouring. Stir till

Mango Kulfi

Serves : 6

4 large ripe mangoes
3 cups milk
¼ cup sugar
2 teaspoons gelatin
2 tablespoons cold water
½ tablespoon finely chopped pistachios

Wash and peel mangoes, cut off pulp and liquidize. Leave a few pieces of pulp to give a fruity taste to kulfi.

Boil milk with sugar, keeping on low heat and stirring all the while till milk is reduced to half its original volume. Remove from heat and set aside. Mix gelatin with cold water and bring to a boil.

Keep stirring, then add to milk and stir well to mix.

Now add mango juice and pulp, and pistachios to milk. Mix well and pour into kulfi cones or a freezing tray. Leave in the freezer for 5 to 6 hours.

Note: You can make any kulfi out of many varieties of fruit, preserved or fresh roots, e.g. mandarin oranges, peaches, even preserved young Chinese ginger.

Sweet Boondi

Serves : 8

1 cup gram *dhal* flour (*besan*)
1 pound (450 g) ghee
¼ teaspoon baking powder
¼ teaspoon saffron
1 cup thin milk
2 pounds (900 g) sugar
6 cups water
1 teaspoon ground cardamom (skinned)

Sift flour into a bowl and rub in 2 teaspoons ghee, baking powder and saffron. Gradually add thin milk and beat well with a wooden spoon to get a soft batter. Set batter aside and make syrup by boiling sugar in 6 cups water till sugar dissolves. Boil for a further 10 minutes till thick enough to leave a coat on a spoon, then turn off heat. Stir in ground cardamom and keep hot.

Heat ghee in a deep frying pan. When smoking hot, hold a spoon with small perforations over the oil. Pour a tablespoonful of batter into this spoon and shake it in short quick movements so that batter falls in drops. Fry for a few minutes till golden brown, then lift out fried boondi with another perforated spoon, drain well and toss into hot syrup. Continue frying, draining and immersing into syrup till all the batter has been used.

Stir the syrup frequently till cooled to room temperature to make sure the tiny balls do not stick together, then lift out boondi balls. Another way of making boondi is to immerse it in a concentrated hot salt and ground chilli solution instead of syrup, then cool, take out to dry and store. Here it becomes a savoury titbit to take at teatime.

Cashew-nut Flaffy

Baking : *20 mins.*
Oven setting : *150°C, 300°F, Gas Regulo 4*
Serves : *6*

¾ cup plain white flour
¼ pound (110 g) butter
¼ cup castor sugar
2 tablespoons thin milk
a few drops of vanilla essence *or* any essence
  desired
1 teaspoon baking powder
2 eggs, beaten
⅛ cup chopped cashew-nuts
extra flour for dusting work surface
extra butter for greasing tray

Warm flour in a slow oven or a clean dry pan over low heat, then sift and leave to cool. Cream butter with sugar, milk and essence. Gradually add flour, baking powder and beaten egg. Knead well for 10 minutes.

Roll out dough on a lightly floured sur-

face to ⅛ inch (¼ cm) thickness. Use decorative cutters to cut out into shapes desired and place on a greased tray (remember to leave room for expansion). Bake in a moderate oven for 20 minutes or till light brown. Cool before storing.

Pineapple Pudding

Baking : *45 mins.*
Oven setting : *150°C, 300°F, Gas Regulo 4*
Serves : *6*

¼ cup cornflour
¼ teaspoon salt
¼ cup castor sugar
2 eggs
¼ cup evaporated milk
1 tablespoon lemon juice
¼ cup pineapple juice
¼ cup drained, crushed pineapple

Warm the flour in a clean, dry pan over very low heat. Stir while warming. Sieve into a bowl and mix with salt and sugar. Beat egg yolks and whites separately.

Mix egg yolks, milk, lemon juice, pineapple juice and crushed pineapple in a large bowl and gradually stir in flour mixture with a wooden spoon. Fold in stiffly beaten egg whites and pour into a heatproof pudding bowl. Stand the bowl in a shallow dish of water and bake in a moderately hot oven for 45 minutes or till set.

Cool to room temperature before serving with cream.

Cold Apricot Pudding

Serves : 6

½ pint apricot puree
½ pint heavy double cream
1 tablespoon boiled gelatin
¼ cup lemon juice
2 tablespoons brandy
1 drop orange colouring
sugar to taste (castor)

Make apricot puree by lightly mashing canned apricots but puree must not be too thick. Fold lightly whipped cream and gelatin into puree. Then add lemon juice, brandy and colour. Sweeten to taste and set in freezer trays till firm. Serve with cubed fruits.

Mango Soufflé

Serves : 6

2 egg whites
4 tablespoons castor sugar
4 teaspoons gelatin
¼ cup water
4 ripe mangoes
1 cup cream

Beat egg whites with sugar till stiff. Dissolve gelatin in hot water. Cut one mango into small pieces and mash the pulp of the other mangoes. Mix mango pulp with cream and beat till stiff. Pour stiffened cream and mango mixture into melted gelatin and add egg white and mango pieces. Pour the mixture into a bowl and refrigerate for at least 6 hours before serving.

Lemon or Orange Soufflé

Serves : 6

2 lemons *or* oranges
3 eggs
4 tablespoons castor sugar
2 tablespoons gelatin
¼ cup water
½ cup cream
2 tablespoons biscuit crumbs

Grate lemon or orange rind to obtain about 1 tablespoon grated rind, then extract juice. Mix juice, grated rind, beaten egg yolks and sugar in a saucepan. Cook over low heat till the mixture thickens. This should take about 10 minutes. Pour mixture into a soufflé dish and set aside.

Dissolve gelatin in hot water and whip with cream and egg whites. Pour onto the cooked mixture in the soufflé dish. Sprinkle biscuit crumbs on top and refrigerate for about 6 hours before serving.

Orange Cups

Serves : 6

6 large oranges
6 tablespoons sugar
2 tablespoons jelly powder (any flavour)
2 cups evaporated milk
1 tablespoon custard powder
vanilla ice-cream
1 tablespoon chopped almonds

Soak oranges in boiling water for 10 minutes. This makes it easier to extract the flesh. Dry them and slice off the tops. Scoop out the flesh and squeeze the juice. Strain the juice.

Mix juice with 1½ cups cold water. Add 2 tablespoons sugar to juice and bring to a boil. Lower heat and let it simmer for 5 minutes. Then remove from heat, add jelly powder, stir well and fill about a quarter of each orange cup with jelly.

Add a little milk to custard powder, stir to mix well, then add the rest of the milk and sugar. Bring to a boil, then lower heat and simmer till mixture thickens. Pour over jelly in orange cups till cups are three-quarters full. Refrigerate to set. Just before serving, top the cups with vanilla ice-cream and sprinkle liberally with chopped almonds. Stick a crisp sprig of mint leaves in the ice-cream tops to decorate the cups.

Watermelon Sherbet

Serves : 8

1 watermelon, about 2 pounds (900 g)
1 cup sugar
1 tablespoon lemon juice
few lemon slices

Scoop out the pink pulp of the watermelon and mash it in a bowl. Add sugar to taste, water and lemon juice and chill in the refrigerator.

Serve in tall glasses with a slice of lemon.

Mango Sherbet

Serves : 8

3 tablespoons almonds
1 tablespoon raisins
3 large unripe mangoes
6 cups water
sugar to taste
¼ teaspoon salt
1 teaspoon mango essence
ice-cream (any flavour)

Soak almonds in water for 3 hours to soften. Remove skin and grind with raisins till very smooth. Cook mangoes under a grill, turning occasionally, till pulp is very soft and the skin is charred.

This should take about 20 minutes. Remove mangoes from grill and let them cool.

Skin mangoes and scrape out pulp. Mash it and mix with 6 cups water, sugar to taste, salt and ground almonds and raisins. Add mango essence and beat well. Refrigerate and serve with a scoop of ice-cream.

Note: Green mangoes have been found to contain Vitamin A. It is believed to have a greatly "cooling" effect on "overheated" bodies (the Chinese call it "heatiness").

Savouries

Mutton Kachuri

Serves : 20

Pastry
2 pounds (900 g) plain white flour
1 teaspoon baking powder
1 teaspoon salt
3 tablespoons melted ghee
2 egg whites, beaten

Filling
3 cups melted ghee *or* oil
½ pound (225 g) small potatoes, peeled and
    cubed
1 pound (450 g) minced mutton
4 cloves garlic, chopped
3 onions, finely sliced
1 teaspoon ginger juice
½ tablespoon ground chilli
1 teaspoon sugar
salt to taste
3 teaspoons chopped coriander leaves
1 teaspoon *garam masala*
1 teaspoon roasted ground cummin

Make the pastry dough first. Sift flour with baking powder and salt into a large bowl. Rub in melted ghee and egg whites. Slowly add cold water, kneading well to obtain a soft dough. Cover with a damp tea towel and set aside for 2-3 hours.

Heat ¼ cup ghee or oil in a pan over medium heat and fry potato cubes till light brown. Remove with a slotted spoon to a dish. In the same hot oil, add minced mutton, garlic, onions, ginger juice, chilli, sugar and salt to taste. Stir-fry for 10 minutes, then add ½ cup water, stir well, lower heat and cover the pan.

When mutton is tender, add fried potatoes, coriander leaves, *garam masala* and roasted ground cummin. Cook till dry and remove from heat.

Divide dough into small balls of about 1 ½ inch (4 cm) diameter. Flatten slightly and roll out on a lightly floured surface to a circle of ⅛ (¼ cm) thickness. Put a spoonful of fried mutton in the centre, leaving about 1 inch (2 ½ cm) all round at the edge uncovered. Dampen the edge and draw in towards the centre. Pinch to seal. Now dust with flour and roll out again, but very quickly, so as not to squeeze out the filling. This time you will get a smaller but thicker circle.

Heat remaining ghee or oil in a deep frying pan over low heat and fry kachuris a few at a time till golden brown. Drain well and serve with tamarind *chutney*.

Cauliflower Kachuri

Serves : 20

Pastry
as for Mutton Kachuri

Filling
1 pound (450 g) cauliflower
½ pound (225 g) potatoes
3 cups melted ghee *or* oil
½ teaspoon black cummin
salt to taste
2 teaspoons finely chopped chilli
1 teaspoon *garam masala*
1 teaspoon ground black pepper

Make pastry dough as for Mutton Kachuri and set aside under a damp tea towel for 2-3 hours.

Cut cauliflower into small pieces. Peel and cube potatoes. Heat ¼ cup oil or ghee in a pan over medium heat. When oil is smoking, add black cummin seeds.

After 20 seconds, add cauliflower, potatoes and a little salt. Toss vegetables in oil for 5 minutes, then add ground chilli, sugar and ½ cup water. Stir, cover pan and cook till vegetables are tender and moisture has been absorbed. Turn off heat and stir in *garam masala* and black pepper.

Roll out lumps of dough as for Mutton Kachuri, filling with fried vegetables. Draw in the edges, seal and roll out gently. Deep-fry till golden brown. Serve with chilli and tomato sauces.

Note: 2 tablespoons green peas may be added if desired.

Peanut Kachuri

Serves : 10

Pastry
1 pound (450 g) plain white flour
½ teaspoon baking powder
½ teaspoon salt
2 tablespoons melted butter

Filling
½ pound (225 g) roasted peanuts, ground
6 green chillies, chopped
2 teaspoons chopped coriander leaves
1 tablespoon lemon juice
½ teaspoon sugar
salt to taste
2 cups melted ghee *or* oil

Make pastry dough as for Mutton Kachuri, (page 107), this time using butter instead of ghee. Cover with a damp tea towel and set aside for 2-3 hours.

Mix ground peanuts with chillies, coriander leaves, lemon juice, sugar and salt to taste. Roll out dough as for Mutton Kachuri and fill with peanut mixture. Draw in the edges, seal and roll out gently. Deep-fry till golden brown and serve with mango *chutney* or tomato sauce.

Peas Kachuri

Serves : 20

Pastry
2 pounds (900 g) plain white flour
1 teaspoon baking powder
1 teaspoon salt
3 tablespoons melted ghee

Filling
1 pound (450 g) green peas
½ teaspoon sweet cummin
4 onions, sliced
½ tablespoon ground chilli
1 teaspoon sugar
3 teaspoons chopped coriander leaves
2 teaspoons roasted ground cummin
salt to taste
3 cups melted ghee *or* oil

Make pastry dough as for Mutton Kachuri, (p. 107), this time leaving out egg whites. Set aside for 2-3 hours under a damp tea towel.

Heat 1 tablespoon ghee or oil in a pan over medium heat and stir-fry cummin seeds and sliced onions for 5 minutes. Add peas, ground chilli, sugar, salt and coriander leaves and fry till dry. Stir in roasted ground cummin and remove from heat. Mash these ingredients.

Roll out dough as for Mutton Kachuri, filling with a spoonful of fried peas. Draw in the eggs and seal. Roll out gently and deep-fry till golden brown. Drain well and serve with *chutney.*

Dhal Kachuri

Serves : 20

Pastry
2 pounds (900 g) white flour
1 teaspoon baking powder
1 teaspoon salt
3 tablespoons melted ghee

Filling
½ pound (225 g) *Urhad dhal* (black split beans)
2 cups melted ghee *or* oil
½ teaspoon sweet cummin
4 onions, sliced
4 green chillies, chopped
1 teaspoon sugar
salt to taste
½ tablespoon ground chilli
2 teaspoons ginger juice
1 teaspoon roasted ground cummin
1 teaspoon roasted ground black cummin
2 teaspoons chopped coriander leaves
some rice flour for dusting lumps of dough

Soak *dhal* in water for about 4 hours, then wash and grind to a paste. Make pastry dough as for Mutton Kachuri, (page 107) but without beaten egg. Set aside for 2-3 hours under a damp tea towel.

Heat 1 tablespoon ghee and fry sweet cummin, sliced onions and green chillies for 10 minutes. Add ground *dhal,* sugar, salt, ground chilli, ginger juice, ground cummin, ground black cummin and coriander leaves. Stir-fry for a further 20 minutes, then remove from heat.

Roll out dough as for Mutton Kachuri, this time dusting with rice flour and filling with fried *dhal.* Draw in the edges, seal and roll out gently. Deep-fry till golden brown. Serve with meat or vegetable curries.

Chicken Fuluri

Serves : 8

1 chicken about 2 pounds (900 g)
1 tablespoon yoghurt
1 onion, ground
2 teaspoons ground garlic
2 teaspoons ground ginger
3 teaspoons ground chilli
1 teaspoon soy sauce
1 teaspoon sugar
salt to taste
oil for deep-fat frying
1 small cucumber, peeled and sliced
2 tomatoes, sliced into rings.

Batter
¾ cup self-raising flour, sifted
¾ cup thin milk *or* water
1 teaspoon pepper
½ teaspoon salt
1 egg, beaten
2 teaspoons ginger juice

Cut chicken into small pieces, wash and leave on a clean tea towel to dry. Marinate chicken in a mixture of yoghurt, onion, garlic, ginger, chilli, soy sauce and sugar. Leave chicken in marinade for 4 hours, turning the pieces once every hour. In the meantime, make a soft batter with flour, milk or water, pepper, salt, beaten egg and ginger juice.

Heat oil for deep-fat frying over medium heat. When oil is smoking hot, lower heat. Dip pieces of chicken into batter and fry till golden brown. Drain well and serve with cucumber and tomato slices.

Coconut Fuluri

Serves : 8

1 pound (450 g) grated coconut
4 green chillies, finely chopped
1 onion, finely chopped
3 teaspoons finely chopped coriander leaves
scant ½ cup cornflour *or* rice flour
1 tablespoon plain flour
salt to taste
1 cup oil

Mix coconut with chillies, onion, coriander leaves, both types of flour and salt. Mould into balls of 1 ½ inch (4 cm) diameter and flatten with the palms of your hands. Heat oil over low heat and fry a few pieces at a time till golden brown. Serve with any *chutney.*

Yam Ball Fuluri

Serves : 10

1 pound (450 g) yam *without* stem and skin
¼ pound (110 g) shrimps, shelled and ground
1 onion, finely chopped
4 green chillies, finely chopped
2 teaspoons chopped coriander leaves
1 teaspoon roasted ground cummin
scant ½ cup cornflour *or* rice flour
½ teaspoon sugar
salt to taste
2 cups oil

Cut yam into small pieces. Wash and spread out on a flat heatproof dish. Steam over vigorously boiling water till tender. Remove from heat and mash with a fork when cool.

Mix mashed yam with all the ingredients listed except oil. Make 1 inch (2 ½ cm) balls from the mixture. Heat oil in a pan over medium heat and fry yam balls till golden brown. Serve with any *chutney*. The mashed yam may be made into oblong shapes, if desired.

Eggplant Pur Bhaji

Serves : 10

4 large eggplants
salt to taste
2 cups oil

Batter
¾ cup gram *dhal* flour (*besan*), sifted
6 teaspoons rice flour, sifted (*or* cornflour)
1 egg, beaten
1 tablespoon onion juice
2 teaspoons ginger juice
2 teaspoons ground chilli
1 teaspoon ground turmeric
1 teaspoon sugar
1 teaspoon salt
2 teaspoons poppy seeds

Cut eggplants into 6 pieces, lengthwise (from the stem). Wash, dry and rub with a little salt.

Mix *dhal* flour with rice or cornflour in a large bowl. Make a well in the centre and add beaten eggs, onion juice, ginger juice, ground chilli, ground turmeric, sugar and salt. Slowly, work flour in this well, rubbing with the fingers. When well mixed, add sufficient cold water to make a soft, thick batter. Beat well with a wooden spoon, making sure there are no lumps. Add poppy seeds to the batter.

Heat oil in a pan over medium heat. Dip pieces of eggplant in the batter and fry a few at a time till dark brown. Drain well and serve hot at tea-time or cocktails.

111

Cauliflower Pur Bhaji

Serves : 8

1 pound (450 g) cauliflower
1 teaspoon ground turmeric
salt to taste
2 cups oil

Batter
¾ cup gram *dhal* flour (*besan*), sifted
¾ cup self-raising flour, sifted
2 teaspoons ginger juice
1 tablespoon ground chilli
1 teaspoon cummin
1 teaspoon sugar
2 teaspoons salt

Cut cauliflower into small pieces, wash and dry by pressing gently with paper towel or clean tea towel. Rub with ground turmeric and salt. Set aside for 1 hour.

Mix both kinds of flour with ginger juice, ground chilli, cummin seeds, sugar and salt. Add sufficient cold water to make a soft thick batter and beat well for 5 minutes. Make sure no lumps of flour remain.

Heat oil in a pan over medium heat. Dip cauliflower pieces in batter and fry a few at a time till golden brown. Drain well and serve with chilli sauce.

Potato Pur Bhaji

Serves : 10

1 pound (450 g) potatoes
1 teaspoon salt
2 cups oil

Batter
1½ cups gram *dhal* flour (*besan*), sifted
2 tablespoons self-raising flour *or* rice flour, sifted
1 teaspoon baking powder
1 tablespoon onion juice
2 teaspoons ginger juice
½ tablespoon ground chilli
1 teaspoon sugar
1 teaspoon salt

Slice potato thinly into round shapes. Make a weak salt solution and soak the slices for 1 hour, then drain and leave on a tea towel to dry.

Mix gram *dhal* flour with rice flour, baking powder, onion juice, ginger juice, ground chilli, sugar and salt. Add sufficient cold water to make a soft thick batter and beat well for 5 minutes, making sure no lumps of flour remain.

Heat oil in a pan over low heat. Dip potato slices in batter and fry till the slices rise in oil and are light brown. Drain well and serve hot with fried onion rings and sauce.

Cauliflower Samosa

Serves : 8

Pastry
1 pound (450 g) plain white flour
1 teaspoon baking powder
1 teaspoon salt
3 tablespoons melted ghee
2 egg whites, beaten
rice flour for dusting work surface

Filling
Cauliflower Kachuri filling, (page 108)
oil for deep-fat frying

Sift flour, baking powder and salt into a large bowl. Rub in melted ghee and beaten egg whites. Add a little water. Knead for at least 10 minutes to obtain a pliable dough, adding more water (just a few spoonfuls at a time) if necessary.

Divide dough into small lumps and pat each into a ball of about 1½ inch (4 cm) diameter. Flatten slightly and roll out each ball thinly into a circle on a surface lightly floured with rice flour. Cut the circle in half. Put a teaspoon of the filling on one side of each semicircle, leaving the edge clear. Dampen the edge all round and fold over the other side. Pinch the edges together firmly to get a triangle.

When all the samosas are ready, heat oil in a deep pan over medium heat. Deep-fry samosas till golden brown. Drain well and serve hot.

Mutton Samosa

Serves : 8

Pastry
as for Cauliflower Samosa

Filling
½ pound (225 g) potatoes
1 stick cinnamon
5 pods cardamom
3 onions, sliced
5 cloves garlic, finely chopped
2 teaspoons ginger juice
½ tablespoon ground chilli
1 teaspoon sugar
salt to taste
1 pound (450 g) minced mutton
2 eggs, beaten
3 teaspoons chopped coriander leaves
2 teaspoons roasted ground cummin
1 teaspoon *garam masala*
¼ cup oil

Peel and cube potatoes. Heat oil in a pan over medium heat and fry potatoes till slightly browned and translucent. Remove to a dish.

To the same hot oil add cinnamon and cardamom and fry for 30 seconds. Then add onions, garlic and ginger juice. Stir till onions are light brown, then add ground chilli, sugar and salt. Stir for another minute before adding minced mutton. Fry mutton for about 20 minutes. Add 2 cups water, mix well, then cover and cook over low heat for 30 minutes. Stir occasionally to prevent food at the bottom of the pan from burning. Add beaten eggs, chopped coriander leaves, fried potatoes, roasted ground cummin and *garam masala* after 10 minutes. Stir well and fry till mixture is dry.

Make thin circles of dough as for Cauliflower Samosa above and fill semicircles with fried mutton filling. Deep-fry triangles of mutton samosa till golden brown, drain well and serve hot with tamarind *chutney.*

Channa Ghugni Dana

Serves : 8

1 pound (450 g) *channa* with skin (white *kabuli*
  channa)
salt to taste
½ teaspoon sodium bicarbonate *or* baking powder
½ pound (225 g) minced mutton
½ cup melted ghee *or* oil
2 teaspoons chopped ginger
4 cloves garlic, chopped
4 onions, sliced
3 small potatoes, peeled and cubed
2 tablespoons finely cut coconut
1 tablespoon ground chilli
4 teaspoons roasted ground cummin
2 tablespoons tomato puree
1 teaspoon sugar
4 teaspoons lemon juice
2 teaspoons roasted ground black cummin
3 teaspoons chopped coriander leaves

Soak *channa dhal* in water overnight. Then wash and put in a saucepan with 1 teaspoon salt, sodium bicarbonate and 6 cups water. Bring to a boil, then lower heat and simmer till tender for about 2 hours. If a pressure cooker is used, simmer for about 30 to 40 minutes. Drain and put aside.

Boil minced mutton with 1 teaspoon salt in 2 cups water till dry. Put this aside.

Heat ghee or oil in a pan over medium heat and add ginger, garlic, onions and potatoes. Stir for about 20 minutes, then pour in coconut and fry till light brown. Then add ground chilli, roasted ground cummin, tomato puree, sugar, boiled mutton and boiled *channa dhal.*

Mix well and season to taste. When potato cubes are tender, add lemon juice and black cummin. Remove from heat and stir in chopped coriander leaves.

Serve hot between triangles of crisp toast secured by toothpicks. Alternatively, serve with *pani puri.*

Poached Egg Cutlet

Serves : 6

6 eggs
¼ cup white vinegar
1 teaspoon salt
1 teaspoon pepper
3 teaspoons melted butter
4 green chillies, finely chopped
oil for deep-fat frying
6 pineapple cubes
6 tomato slices

Batter
¾ cup plain white flour
1 egg, beaten
⅔ cups milk
1 teaspoon salt
1 teaspoon pepper
3 teaspoons melted butter
scant ½ cup warm water

Bring 10 cups of water to a boil with vinegar in a large saucepan. (The vinegar helps to firm egg whites.) Lower heat and let the water simmer very gently.

Break 1 egg into a cup and, bringing the cup as close to the surface of boiling water as possible, slide the egg into the water. Watch to see which part of the water is simmering. Slide your egg in there so that the bubbles slow down the descent of the egg, giving the egg white a longer time to firm up before reaching the bottom where it may stick. Do the same with the other 5 eggs, as quickly as possible, so that cooking time is almost the same for all the eggs. When all the eggs are in water, run a slotted spoon through the water at the surface to move the water (and eggs) gently.

After 5 minutes, lift out a poached egg with a slotted spoon and press gently to check firmness of the yolk. If firm, remove all eggs to a pan of ice-cold water to cool and wash away vinegar.

Trim off ragged white edges and leave poached eggs in a mixture of salt, pepper, melted butter and chopped green chillies for 30 minutes, turning them once during this time.

Make the batter by combining flour, beaten egg, milk, salt, pepper and melted butter. Add a little water to give a thick soft batter. Beat well for 20 minutes, making sure no lumps of flour remain.

Heat oil in a deep pan over medium heat. Dip poached eggs one at a time in batter and deep-fry till golden brown. Serve each on a long pick with a pineapple cube and a slice of tomato.

Creamed Fish Fries

Serves : 8

1 pound (450 g) fillet of threadfin (*ikan kurau*),
  skinned
2 teaspoons salt
3 teaspoons finely chopped parsley
2 teaspoons lemon juice
oil for deep-fat frying
some pineapple cubes
some small pieces of crisp lettuce

Batter
scant 1 cup plain white flour
¼ teaspoon salt
1 teaspoon pepper
½ cup cream
1 tablespoon melted butter
¼ cup grated cheese
4 green chillies, ground
½ cup milk
a little warm water (if necessary)

Cut fish into 1-inch (2½ cm) squares. Marinate the pieces in a mixture of salt, parsley and lemon juice for 2 hours.

Make the batter by mixing flour, baking powder, salt, pepper, cream, melted butter, cheese, ground chillies and gradually stirring in milk and a little warm water to make a soft thick batter. Beat well for 20 minutes.

Heat oil in a deep pan over medium heat. Dip fish in batter and deep-fry till light brown. Drain and serve each piece of fish on a pick with a pineapple cube and a folded-over piece of lettuce.

Sago Pillau

Serves : 10

½ pound (225 g) pearl sago
2 potatoes
1 pound (110 g) roasted peanuts
4 dried chillies
½ teaspoon mustard seed
2 onions, sliced
4 green chillies, chopped
2 tablespoons grated coconut
2 teaspoons chopped coriander leaves
1 teaspoon sugar
salt to taste
3 tablespoons melted ghee *or* oil

Soak sago in water for an hour, then wash by rubbing fistfuls of it together and drain well. Put aside. Boil potatoes till almost cooked, then peel and cut into small pieces. Pound roasted peanuts coarsely.

Heat ghee or oil in a pan over medium heat and fry dried chillies, mustard seed, onions and green chillies for 5 minutes, stirring continuously. Then add potatoes and stir till slightly brown. Add sago seeds, coconut, peanuts, coriander leaves, sugar and salt. Fry for 20 minutes, stirring thoroughly all the time, then remove from heat. Serve with a *chutney* in small individual dishes.

116

Pani Puri

Serves : 8

2 teaspoons sweet cummin
1 ½ cups plain white flour
¼ cup rice flour
1 teaspoon ground black pepper
2 teaspoons salt
2 teaspoons sugar
¼ teaspoon baking soda
1 tablespoon lemon juice
2 teaspoons ginger juice
ghee for deep-fat frying

Soak sweet cummin seeds in 1 cup water for about 4 hours.

Put plain flour, rice flour, pepper, salt, sugar and baking soda in a bowl. Combine well with 3 tablespoons melted ghee. Add lemon juice, ginger juice and strained sweet cummin juice. Knead well for about 10 minutes. The dough should have the consistency of bread dough. Add a few teaspoonfuls of water if it is too hard and a little flour if it is too soft. Cover the dough with a damp tea towel and let it rest for 3 hours.

Divide dough into little lumps and mould into balls the size of small marbles. Roll out into thin circles on a lightly floured surface, using a rolling pin dusted with flour. Place rolled out circles of dough neatly on a large tray covered with a damp cloth as the rest are being rolled out. When ready to fry, take the ones rolled out at the start first.

Heat ghee in a deep pan and when smoking hot, place 2 puris in the oil. Immediately, scoop up some hot oil and splash over puris. Do this a few times to make them puff up. When golden brown, remove them from oil with a slotted spoon and drain on some paper towels. Cool on a wire rack and store in airtight tins till ready for serving.

Serve pani puri with potato curry and tamarind *chutney*. Using a finger, poke a hole in one side and put in a teaspoonful of one or the other, or both.

Cheese Guli

Serves : 8

¼ cup grated cheese
2 cups plain white flour
½ teaspoon baking powder
⅛ cup castor sugar
1 egg, beaten
¼ teaspoon salt
½ cup milk
2 tablespoons cornflour
oil for deep-fat frying
2 tomatoes, sliced

In a large bowl, mix cheese with plain flour, baking powder, castor sugar, beaten egg and salt. Add milk a little at a time and rub with the fingers till a soft dough is obtained. Shape into balls the size of small marbles and coat with cornflour. Deep-fry over low heat to a golden brown. Serve garnished with tomato slices.

Bird's nests for Cheese Guli — A charming way to serve cheese guli is in "bird's nests" made out of shredded spring onion. Shred spring onions finely and soak in iced water. This softens the spring onion. Leave for 3 hours, then dry and arrange into nests. To serve, place 4 cheese gulis in each nest. Arrange the nests on a dish with tomato slices.

Potato Guli

Serves : 8

6 large potatoes, boiled, peeled and mashed
6 teaspoons cornflour
6 green chillies, chopped
3 teaspoons chopped coriander leaves
2 teaspoons chopped mint leaves
4 teaspoons poppy seeds
1 tablespoon finely ground coconut
1 teaspoon sugar
salt to taste
oil for deep-fat frying

Mix mashed potatoes with cornflour, chilli, coriander leaves, mint leaves, poppy seeds, coconut, sugar and salt. Mould small portions of the mixture into balls the size of large marbles and deep-fry them over low heat till golden brown. Serve with tomato sauce or tamarind *chutney*.

Top — Plain Pillau
Bottom — Mutton Rib Cutlet
Bottom — Tomato Chutney (left)
Chicken Cutlet (right)
(Recipes: pp. 1, 28, 82, for Chicken Cutlet, see recipe for Mutton Cutlet, p. 30)

Top left — Lalmohon
Top right — Watermelon Sherbet
Bottom — Kheer Kamala
(Recipes: pp. 100, 106, 99)

(clockwise) — Tea, Kulfi, Cheese Guli, Prawn Guli
(Recipes: pp. 101, 118, 123)

Top plate: (clockwise)
Ginger, Almonds, Clove, Star Anise, Turmeric, Dry Chilli, Cardamom, Bay leaves, Cinnamon sticks
Bottom plate: (clockwise)
Sweet cummin, Kunyit powder, Fenugreek, Cummin seed powder, Small cummin seeds, Mustard seeds,
Coriander seeds, Chilli powder.

Egg Guli

Serves : 12

6 eggs, hardboiled
4 green chillies, seeded and finely chopped
2 teaspoons finely chopped coriander leaves
1 onion, finely chopped
5 teaspoons cornflour
salt to taste
oil
4 tablespoons grated cheese
2 teaspoons roasted ground cummin
2 teaspoons lemon juice
20 roasted cashewnuts, ground
some toothpicks
some lettuce leaves, shredded

Trim off the ends of hardboiled eggs so that you can sit them, then halve widthwise. Remove the yolks and mash with chillies, coriander leaves, onion, cornflour and salt. Add a little water to obtain a binding dough. Mould into small balls and fry a few at a time in shallow oil over low heat till light brown. Leave in a colander to drain.

Mix grated cheese, roasted ground cummin, lemon juice and ground cashewnut in a bowl. Divide the mixture into 12 equal portions and use a teaspoon to stuff each egg white with one cheese portion. Spear egg gulis with toothpicks and stick them into the egg white cups. Serve on a bed of lettuce shreds, garnished with shredded red chillies.

Prawn Guli

Serves : 8

½ pound (225 g) shrimps, shelled
2 teaspoons ground chilli
1 slice bread without crust, soaked and shredded
1 egg, beaten
1 tablespoon roasted ground peanuts
1 onion, finely chopped
2 teaspoons plain white flour
2 teaspoons chopped coriander leaves
½ teaspoon sugar
salt to taste
2 tablespoons cornflour
oil for deep-fat frying
2 turnips
2 pieces of lettuce leaves
a few toothpicks

Pound shrimps coarsely and mix with chilli, bread, egg, peanuts, onion, flour, coriander leaves, sugar and salt to taste.

Knead to mix well and take up a small lump at a time and pat into a ball, the size of a marble and shaped like a mushroom. Coat with cornflour and deep-fry over low heat till brown. Serve with any salad.

Decoration: Cut a turnip into the shape of a bowl and spread lettuce leaves in it. Prick each guli with a toothpick and stick each onto the outside of the "bowl" like a mushroom growing on the "bowl".

123

Guli Kabab

Serves : 8

1 pound (450 g) minced mutton *or* pork
4 teaspoons yoghurt
1 teaspoon ground garlic
1 onion, ground
2 teaspoons ground chilli
1 teaspoon ground ginger
3 teaspoons chopped coriander leaves
½ teaspoon sugar
salt to taste
2 slices bread
4 teaspoons plain white flour
1 teaspoon roasted ground cummin
some toothpicks
2 eggs, beaten
breadcrumbs
oil for deep-fat frying
2 cucumbers, peeled and cubed
some lettuce leaves, shredded
2 tomatoes, sliced into rings

Marinate minced meat in a mixture of yoghurt, ground garlic, onion, chilli and ginger, finely chopped coriander leaves, sugar and salt to taste. Set aside for 2 hours. At the same time, remove crust from bread slices and soak in water.

Squeeze water out of bread and shred. Add flour, minced meat mixture and roasted ground cummin. Mix well and divide into small round portions about the size of large marbles. Elongate and pat into oblong shapes. Insert a toothpick into one end of each oblong, dip in beaten egg and coat with breadcrumbs. Deep-fry over low heat till golden brown.

Spread shredded lettuce on a flat dish and arrange tomato slices and cucumber cubes on lettuce. Stick guli kabab onto cucumber cubes and serve with some tomato and chilli sauce, either at cocktails or teatime.

Menu Suggestions

Lunch

1. Mutton Cutlet
   Madras Fish Curry
   Labra
   Chutney
   Rice
   Watermelon Sherbet

2. Chicken Doh Piazi
   Egg Roll
   Prawn Korma
   Brinjal Kalia
   Plain Pillau
   Orange Cups

Two-dish Meals

1. Tandoori Chicken
   Naan

2. Prawn Pillau
   Madras Fish Curry

3. Seekh Kabab
   Onion Salad

4. Wholemeal Flour Chapati
   Dry Mutton Curry

Dinner

1. Green Chilli Chicken
   Stuffed Cabbage
   Prawn Curry
   Spicy Mutton Soup
   Mango Sambal
   Chutney
   Rice
   Cold Apricot Pudding

2. Lamb with Almonds
   Chicken Korma
   Fish Ferezi
   Cabbage Roll Bhaji
   Chutney
   Rice
   Mango Sherbet

Buffet/Party

Fish Kabab
Tandoori Chicken
Naan
Mutton Rib Cutlet
Bhindi Kari
Seekh Kabab in Pieces
Dry Mutton Curry
Mutton Samosa
Calcutta Paratha
Onion Salad
Sweet Boondi
Pineapple Chutney

The Indian spice rack (basic spices you will need in your kitchen when "cooking Indian") —

bay leaves
black cummin seeds (*jintan hitam*)
black peppercorns, whole and ground
cardamom, whole and ground (*buah pelaga*)
cinnamon sticks (*kayu manis*)
chilli powder
coriander seeds (*ketumbar*)
cummin (*jintan putih*)
curry leaves/powder
cloves, whole and ground (*bunga cingkeh*)
fenugreek, whole seeds and ground (*halba*)
poppy seeds (*kas-kas*)
garam masala
fennel

It is advisable to buy the spices in small quantities and store them in airtight jars in a cool, dry place.

Addresses of Spice Dealers

Singapore

1. Singapore General Store
    60 Serangoon Road Singapore 0820

2. P. Govindasamy Pillai (Singapore Ltd)
    46 Serangoon Road Singapore 0820

United Kingdom

1. Fortnum & Mason Ltd
    181 Piccadilly London W1

2. Harrods (Food Dept.)
    Knightsbridge, London S.W.1.

3. Army & Navy Stores
    105 Victoria St. London S.W.1.

4. John Little & Son
    Eastgate Row, Chester